50th Reunion

MARIAN
HIGH SCHOOL

Class of 1974

Published 2024 – KDP by Amazon.
All Rights Reserved.
ISBN: 9798336752021

Dedication

*Dedicated to the families who raised us,
the teachers who shaped us,
and the classmates who shared four years with us.*

Our thoughts and prayers are with those who left us too soon.

Ann O'Brien

Christine Johnson Koopman

Colleen Kane-Dacri

Deborah Raad

Debra Saunders

Felicia Gulanchenski Cardillo

Kathleen Geran Werner

Linda Dykas

Lindsay Miller

Martha Keenan

Mary Leahey

Maryan Mangini Pappas

Patricia Johnson

Rita Grady Thurston

Rosemary Cooney Schultz

Sheila Grogan Dell'Aquila

Classmate List

ANDREA (LEGACY) CARLSON 10

ANNE CLANCY NEALON 12

ANNE-MARIE CANAVAN BUHRMESTER 14

ANNMARIE HAGGERTY 16

AUDREY ASSELTA DUTREMBLE 18

CAROLANN MARTIN 19

CAROL LOHMAN BRANN 22

CAROL SERETI LITTLE 24

CHRISTINE HARDING TURPIN 28

COLLEEN KANE DACRI 30

DEB SZEREJKO 32

DEE DEE CALLAHAN KOHLER 34

ELIZABETH (BETTY) Z. KARAS HALLINAN 36

ELIZABETH WRIGHT BROWNING 38

ELLEN WOODS RYAN 40

JILL MCGRATH JONES 42

JOAN LADNER MARDIN 44

JOAN METIVIER BERTRAND 46

KATHY HANLON O'CONNELL 48

KATHY HART HARRINGTON 50

KATHY MCMAHON STANSKY	52
KATHY NAUGHTON HEAD	54
KATHY ROBICHAUD BARNARD	56
KAREN RITCHIE IGO	58
LINDA CORRIERE	60
MARGUERITE SAVAGE	62
MARYANN HARRITY BURNS	64
MARY BETH BARNICLE ROCKWELL	66
MARY KEENAN	68
MARY MURPHY BEER	69
MAURA CONLON	70
MAUREEN CORRIGAN ROURKE	72
MAUREEN ERREDE BUMANN	74
MICHELLE O'NEIL ELLIOTT	76
NANCY GARDINER THIBAULT	78
NOREEN LAHAIR DAVIEAU	80
PATTY BOULAY COOK	82
PAULA GARREPY MATTHEW	88
ROSEMARY DEEDY GOODMAN	90
SALLY NAWN HARTMANN	92
STEPHANIE (CULLEN) ABISLA	94
SUSAN ATHY	98
TARYN MCCARTHY	100

TERESA MARY PERODEAU DOYLE	102
THERESE MCKEON LOGAN	104
WENDY CURTIS CLARKE	106

CLASSMATES

Andrea (Legacy) Carlson

ajlegacy@yahoo.com
508-864-0178
Sturbridge, MA

I believe that my time at Marian educated me academically as well as socially. Looking back, I wish I spent more time on books than boys. I graduated from Assumption with a degree in Social Rehabilitation and Psychology even though I always wanted to be a teacher.

So, after working as a vocational counselor for the City of Worcester, meeting and marrying my husband, Ron, and having my only child, Matt, I went back to school to get my Masters in Secondary Education with a concentration in Special Education. I taught at Oxford, Southbridge, and Auburn High Schools for over 32 years.

Upon retirement, I worked for Quinsigamond Community College as a math and science specialist in the GED/HiSet program. I loved every day of every job. My inability to have more than one child was compensated by the many close relationships I have forged with my students and their families. I do miss having a classroom.

In retirement, I get to enjoy more time with my son and his family. Matt is 44 and has been married to Molly for 19 years. Matt was just made principal of Auburn Middle School. They gave me four grandchildren, Liam 16, Phineas 13, Charlotte 10 1/2 and Emilia Rose 8 1/2. My husband is resistant to retirement but tells me it will be on or about June, 2025. I have 2 beautiful doodle dogs and am very close to my brother, Ray, and his family.

We have lived in Sturbridge for 37 years but always claim our roots in the Woo. Ron and I enjoy traveling and an occasional Manhattan or two in the evening.

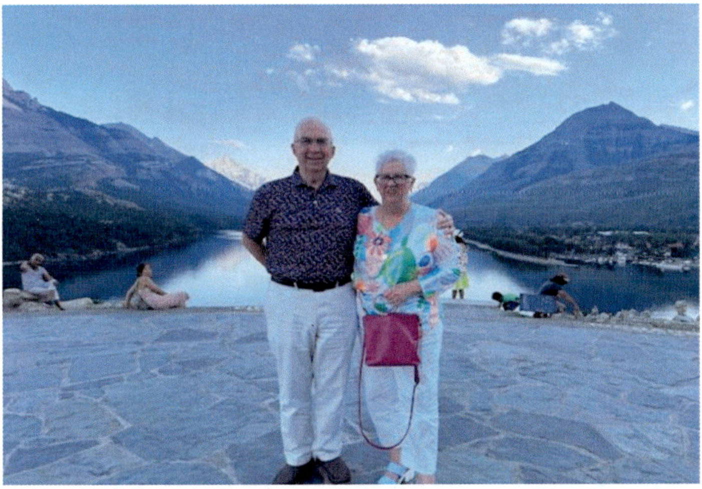

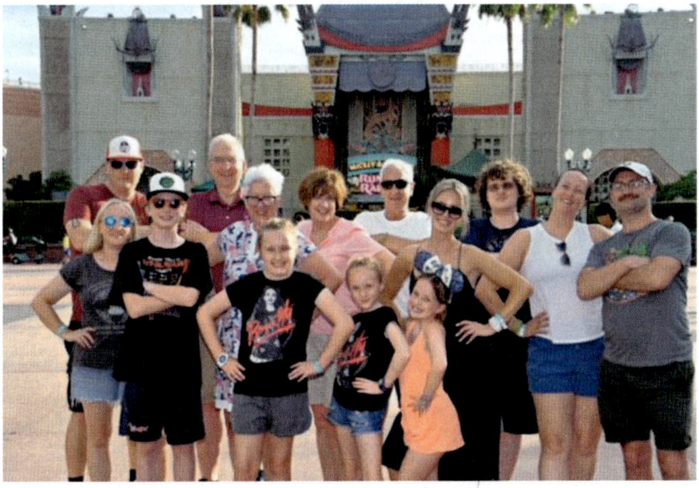

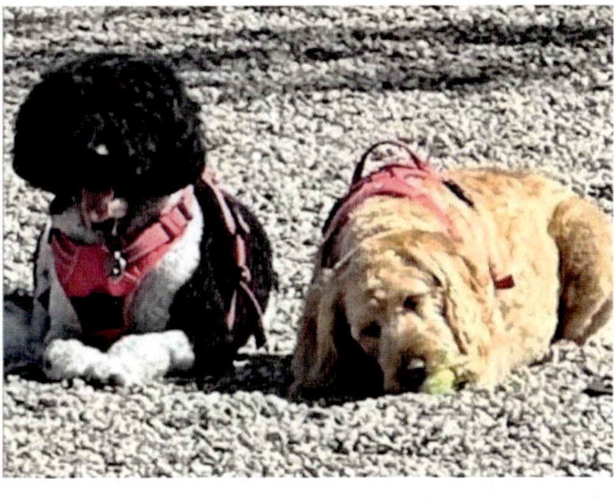

Anne Clancy Nealon

thomas@nealonlaw.com
774-270-0823
Hopkinton, MA

I graduated from American University in Washington, D.C. with a degree in Criminal Justice in 1978. After graduation, I was a social worker in Worcester and Boston. I met my husband, Tom, in 1979 and we got married in 1981. We moved to his hometown of Hopkinton, MA and have lived there for over 40 years.

I left my field, as a social worker, to raise our 6 children, Matthew, Patrick, Callie, Andrew, Jack, and Mary Catherine. I have 7 grandchildren and one on the way. I am a devoted grandmother and enjoy spending time with family and friends.

In the summers, you can find me down the outer Cape!

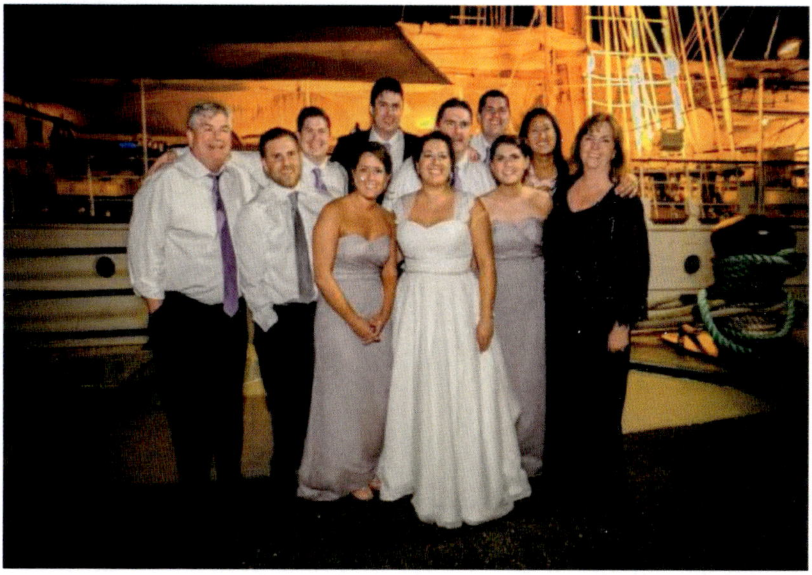

Anne-Marie Canavan Buhrmester

Ambuhrmester@gmail.com
847-505-8948
Waukegan, IL

After Marion, I attended Anna Maria College graduating with a BA in Social Work (1978). I met my husband, Duncan Buhrmester, in the summer of 1975. We married in August 1978, moving to his hometown of Waukegan, Illinois about 40 miles north of Chicago on Lake Michigan. We have raised two children, Daniel (1984) a firefighter/paramedic and 3 years later, Erin (Zyzda) a sales manager for a large food company. We are blessed with 2 granddaughters, Katelynn (10) and Addison (8) and a new grandson, Stephen Roy Zyzda (born this past April).

My work career has varied, I worked as a Social Worker, then stayed home with my children. Once they were in middle school, I returned to work at the YMCA in management until deciding to return to school to get a Master's in teaching with a concentration as a reading specialist along with endorsements in ESL and gifted students. I retired in 2018 to help care for my granddaughter after my son's divorce.

My greatest accomplishment is our family and our many adventures together. While our family returns to Massachusetts often to visit my family, our main adventures take place in Northwoods of Wisconsin where we have enjoyed fishing, boating and everything the lakes have to offer.

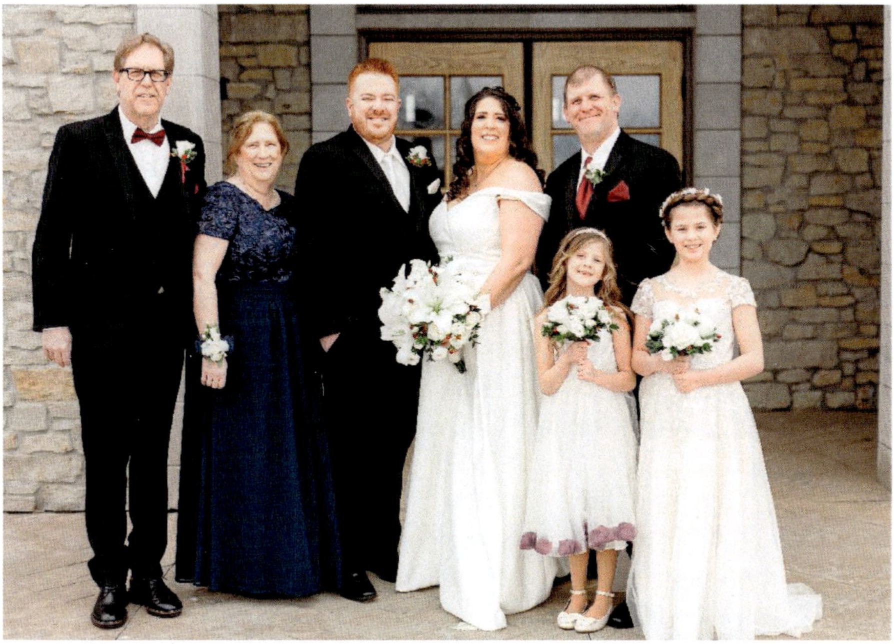

Annmarie Haggerty

haggerty.a35@yahoo.com
annmarie@forgottenfelines.com
Petaluma, CA

After graduating from Marian, I remained in Worcester and worked at several different companies, i.e. , New England Telephone, City of Worcester Health Department, utilizing all the secretarial skills I had been taught at Marian. I got married to my high school sweetheart and started a family. We had 3 daughters, Joann, Beth and Amanda.

In 1981, I re-entered the work force as a PBX operator at Worcester Hahnemann Hospital part time. A year later, I transferred to the Admitting Department, and a year after that, I transferred to the Emergency Department as the Unit Secretary. I stayed at Hahnemann in the ER until it was closed in 1996. I was then offered a similar position at Memorial, the hospital we had merged with in 1994. While working in the ER, I started taking courses at Worcester State College. My major was Media, and I was heavily involved in the Theatre Department. I appeared in all the productions, Shakespeare, Tom Stoppard, Churchill over the 5 years I was a student, and even directed a One Act play. In my senior year, I was nominated for a special national award for drama, called the Irene Ryan award. I participated with actors from all over New England and it was a great experience. I was very proud of my accomplishments at Worcester State College and being a non-traditional student helped me immensely.

I stayed at Hahnemann in the ER until it was closed in 1996. I was then offered a similar position at Memorial, the hospital we had merged with in 1994. We then merged again by buying UMass Hospital. I ended up staying at Memorial in the ER until I retired in 2016.

My three daughters are married and have 6 children between them and 4 grandchildren. I am a proud great-grandmother and come back to Massachusetts often to spend time with them. My marriage ended in 1999 and I found new interests and friendships in a local Elks Lodge I would attend to play Bingo with a friend from work. The Benevolent and Protective Order of Elks was for men only until 1996, when women were allowed to join. So, I did! I became an officer within the first year of membership and was elected to be the first female President of the Worcester Elks in 2001. I met a wonderful man, who was a member of the Auburn Lodge of Elks and we began dating. He decided to run for office and when he became President I transferred to his Lodge. Four years after his Presidency, I became President of that Lodge, as well! I'm very involved in the Elks and am proud to have been promoted to a position which is only granted by the Past National Presidents of the Elks Order.

I moved to Petaluma, California in 2018 to retire (hated it!!!) and live with my middle daughter, her husband and my granddaughter, who now, has graduated from Bates College and is working at UMass Chan Medical School in Worcester as a lab assistant. Life moves in a circle sometimes! I found a position as Administrative Assistant in Santa Rosa, at a non-profit called Forgotten Felines of Sonoma County, and have worked here for over 3 years. It's a very rewarding experience for someone who loves cats as much as I do. Looking forward to seeing everyone "back home"!

Audrey Asselta Dutremble

audreydutremble@yahoo.com
508-826-2747
Worcester, MA

I have been married 45 years to my husband Bob. We have three children and six grandchildren! I worked most of my life in retail and am now retired. Enjoying the Grandchildren and enjoy painting as my hobby.

Carolann Martin

martin.carolann@gmail.com
802-353-4000
Wallingford, VT

I was born to two Worcester natives who met while working at the Worcester VA. They got married and moved to Main South where my father adopted my oldest brother (whose father died at the end of WWII) and then had two sons and one little daughter with my mother. We grew up in a neighborhood where we played outside all day, skated on frozen ponds, and slid down Hickson's Hollow in the winter. Kindergarten at Gates Lane, 1-6 at Our Lady of the Angels and 7-8 at Woodland Prep. And then off to the newest, Catholic, high school in the city.

Marian Central Catholic High School. All girls. A fantastic new home ec kitchen! Way over on the other side of the city. Bus rides or a lot of walking if you missed it. Freshmen were offered a pool pass for the roof for a slight charge. New friends, new teachers, new lunchroom, and dances! Dances with boys!

But the world was changing also. Vietnam War protests, nightly news with disturbing sights of explosions and burning across the world and nuns in street clothes. Riots, presidential crimes, rights for women, rights for sexual freedom, legal abortion, racial equality, and a growth of interest in drugs to escape the chaos. Our music reflected this new world. We, the class of 1974, lived through all of this together.

I attended different colleges. I got married in 1979, then joined the USPS – as the 2nd woman ever hired – in Haverhill, MA. We moved to Vermont in 1985 and worked hard to keep four children fed and entertained with VHS tapes (because we only got three stations with the antenna on the roof). Graduated finally in 1985 with a BA in English Studies. Divorced in 2006. The kids went off to college and now two are married. I have four grandchildren and another little girl coming before the reunion. The family I came from is so dramatically different from the family I have created. We love each other, we like each other and we help each other.

This is my greatest accomplishment in my life! I could die happy any day now, but I really want to hang around and see what's yet to come. I look forward to seeing whoever can come and hearing any news on those who can't make it. See you in September!

21

Carol Lohman Brann

seahorse214@gmail.com
508-446-0238
Lincoln, RI

I graduated from Massachusetts College of Pharmacy (Boston) in 1981. I practiced as a registered pharmacist for 40 years in both the hospital and retail settings in Massachusetts and Rhode Island until my retirement in 2021. I currently reside in Lincoln, Rhode Island with my beagle, Fern Rose.

I am incredibly proud of my 2 children. My daughter, Theresa, lives in Boston and her career is with Winston's Florist. Her passions are in her arts, friends, and travel. My son, Kehan, works in the cannabis industry. His passions are in music, vinyls and bands.

I have always loved baking, sewing/quilting, model trains, gardening, walking with my dog, and being near the ocean. In retirement, I am lucky to have my health and the time to enjoy all these things as well as investing in friends.

Carol Brann, RPh

Carol Lohman

Carol Sereti Little

carolejlittle@gmail.com
281-259-4130
Willis, TX

My husband Keith and I live in Willis, TX with our daughter, Victoria, and our high-maintenance Jack Russell Terrier mix, Charlie. Keith is a middle school Algebra teacher, (yes, Leo, since I could never figure it out, I married someone who can.) Our oldest, Vincent, is 36, married with a 5-year-old little girl and a 2.5-year-old little boy. They live in Elgin, TX (the brisket capital of Texas, just west of Austin. I'm a semi-retired real estate agent and love it.

As for how Marian impacted my life, it's hard to condense it without minimizing what a gift it was. Like too many kids, my home life was always unstable due to divorce, frequent moves, etc. Getting accepted into Marian was a dream come true. I knew it would lead to a better life if I could just stay from start to finish. In my junior year, I became temporarily homeless. A dear friend and her family offered me a place to stay for as long as I needed it, no questions asked. The next day, I found myself waiting for Bishop Rueger outside his office hoping to work out a solution to allow me to stay in school. For a kid who grew up surrounded by adults who said I wasn't smart enough, that I wasn't college material, I didn't have the right background or connections - what happened that day changed my perspective and the course of my life.

Until that day, I never realized how much he and most of the staff at Marian cared about every one of us. His words and support propelled me forward and I never looked back until 2012 when I reached out in a letter to let him know how his support changed the trajectory of my life for the better. We remained in touch right up until the year he passed away.

As much as I would love to be there with you to catch up with each of you and hear where your journeys have taken you, the timing is just not the best right now. I have enjoyed reconnecting with many of you, and look forward to seeing the photos and bios.

As for the staff, Leo, as much as we butted heads, in the end, I knew how much you cared but don't worry, I won't let your secret out. Ms. Castagna, congratulations on your induction into the Hall of Fame - what a career! Your discipline and dedication to fitness were not wasted on me. Your "Drop and give me 10" came in handy when my firstborn entered high school and hormones took over. Needless to say, he was extremely fit by the time he graduated. He's now a CrossFit coach. Mrs. Nader would be proud to know her Spanish tutoring served me well over the last 5 decades. Ms. O'Hearn, your classes expanded my world and filled my imagination with scenes from Shakespeare, Chaucer, and all the many great authors and poets you introduced into my world. Thank you! I wish you all continued blessings and know you're always welcome if you're ever in the area.

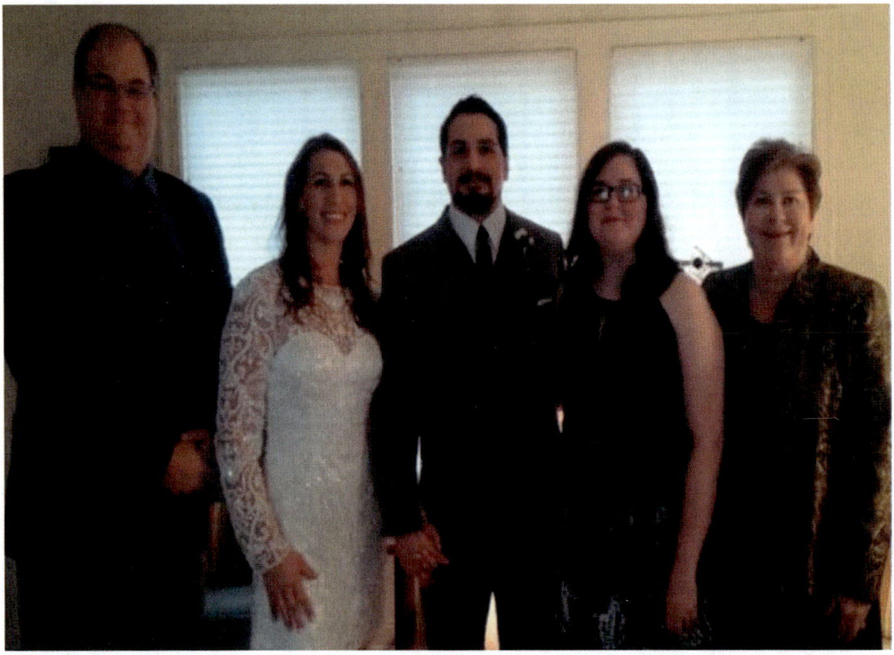

Nothing Great Was Ever Achieved Without Enthusiasm.
-Ralph Waldo Emerson

Christine Harding Turpin

Cristurpin123@gmail.com
1-774-230-1449
Thompson, CT

After graduating from Marian, I attended Quinsigamond Community College and became a dental hygienist. I spent most of my career working in two dental practices, retiring in 2020. I enjoyed working with people on their wellness journey.

In 1975, I met my husband, John, and we were married in 1978. We raised two sons, Mike and Andy. We are blessed with two lovely daughters-in-law, Nikki and Renee. Our three grandkids Caleb, Ella and Gracie complete our family.

I lived in Charlton, MA for over 30 years. Five years ago, we bought a house on a lake in Thompson, CT. I enjoy gardening, kayaking and reading. I love to travel. Some of my favorite places have been Grand Canyon, Belize and Aruba. Looking forward to whatever life brings my way.

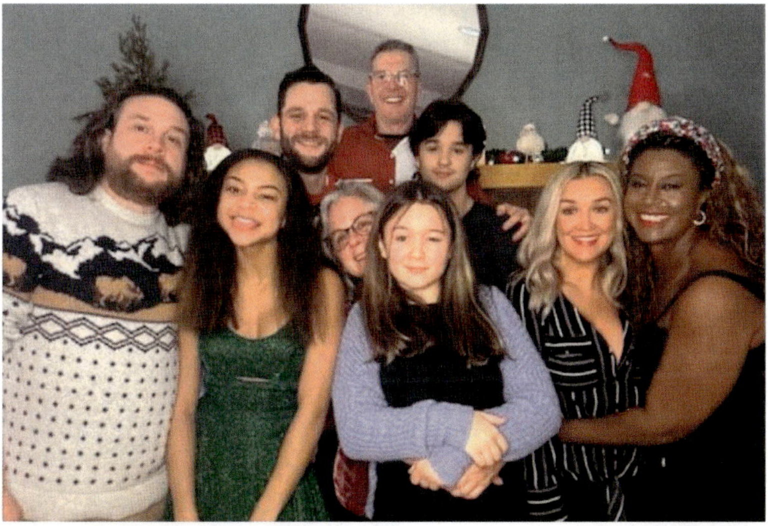

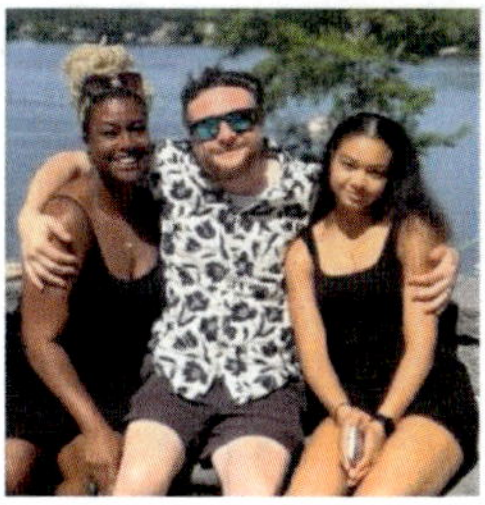

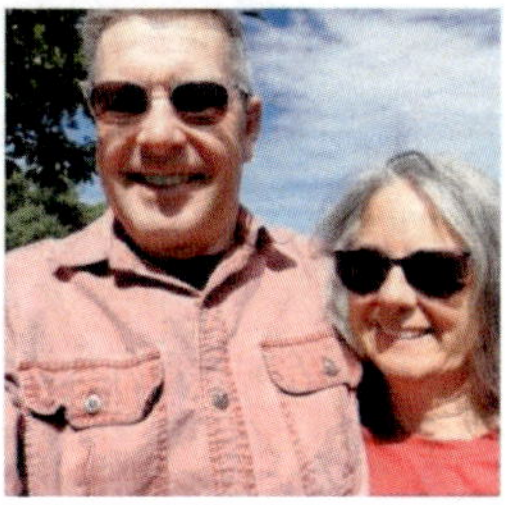

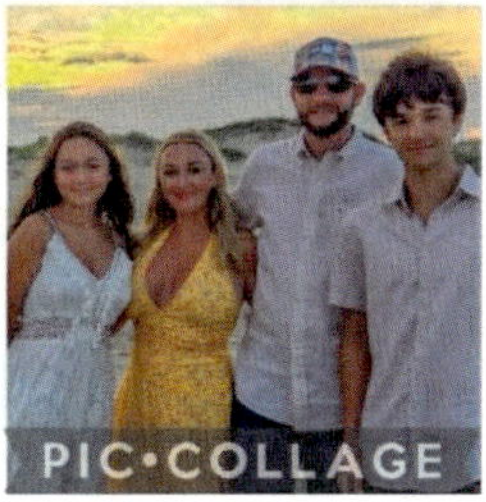
PIC•COLLAGE

Colleen Kane Dacri

(50th Reunion Committee Planner)
Passed Away May 18, 2024

Colleen Mary Rita Kane-Dacri was a force of nature. She was hilarious, fearless, and the life of the party. At times, she could be outrageous but to those of us that knew her best, she was also compassionate, loving and generous. Colleen married her high school sweetheart, James Dacri, and the two of them enjoyed an almost 50 year marriage. In the late 90s, when Colleen was working as a liaison to a Chinese adoption agency, she and James adopted their own baby girl, Lillian. Lily will always be the shining light in Colleen's life.

After living abroad in Germany while James was in the military, they moved to San Francisco where Colleen finished college, went to graduate school and became a licensed psychotherapist in the state of California. She ran her own successful practice in both San Francisco and Marin County for nearly 40 years where she cared for adults, couples, and especially children in crisis. Colleen served on many boards in the Bay Area including Haight Ashbury Free Clinic's Womens Needs Center and the Greenwood School in Mill Valley.

Colleen accomplished so many things in her short time here on earth. She lost her own father at an early age and I think her awareness that life can be too short was what drove her to experience all that she could. She travelled extensively throughout the world, created beautiful art and most importantly, made a huge impression on the people surrounding her. Her memorial service held this past June is a testament to that. Held at her home in Larkspur, CA surrounded by Redwood trees and Jasmine vines, friends from all over gathered in her backyard to celebrate our good fortune in having known her.

Colleen Kane-Dacri

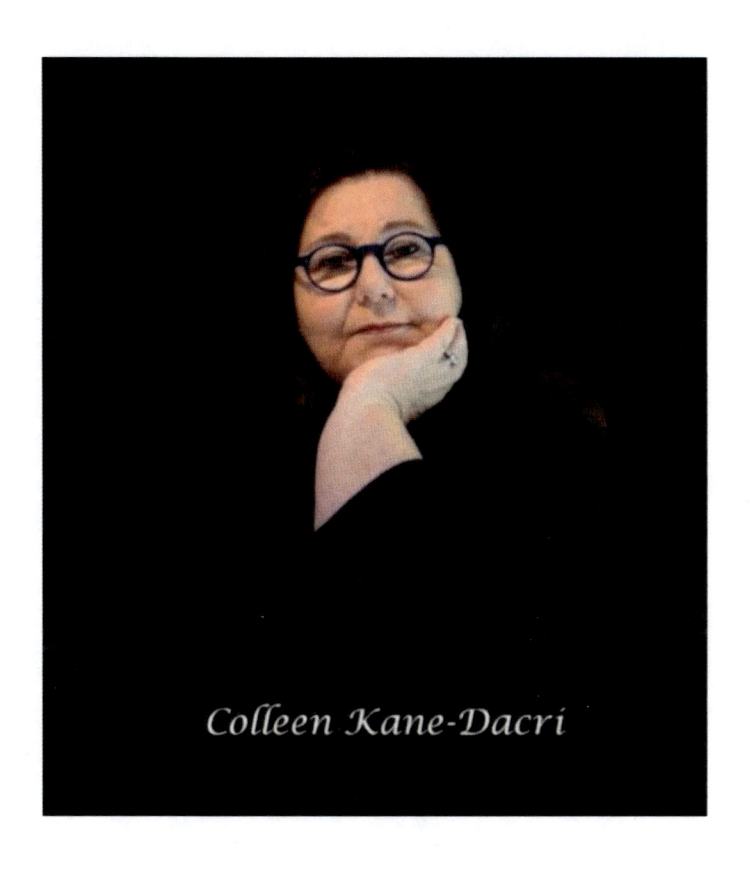

"To live each day is a privilege
So, when you rise each day
Inhale deeply and exhale fully and
Live your day in privilege"
- Colleen Kane Dacri
1955 – 2024

Deb Szerejko

debszrjk@gmail.com
508-579-5847
Worcester, MA

I have 2 sons. Twin grand daughters and a grandson. I have worked for the State for 25 years. That would be the Department of Environmental Protection and I am currently at the Department of Mental Health as a paralegal. I am living in Worcester with two cats.

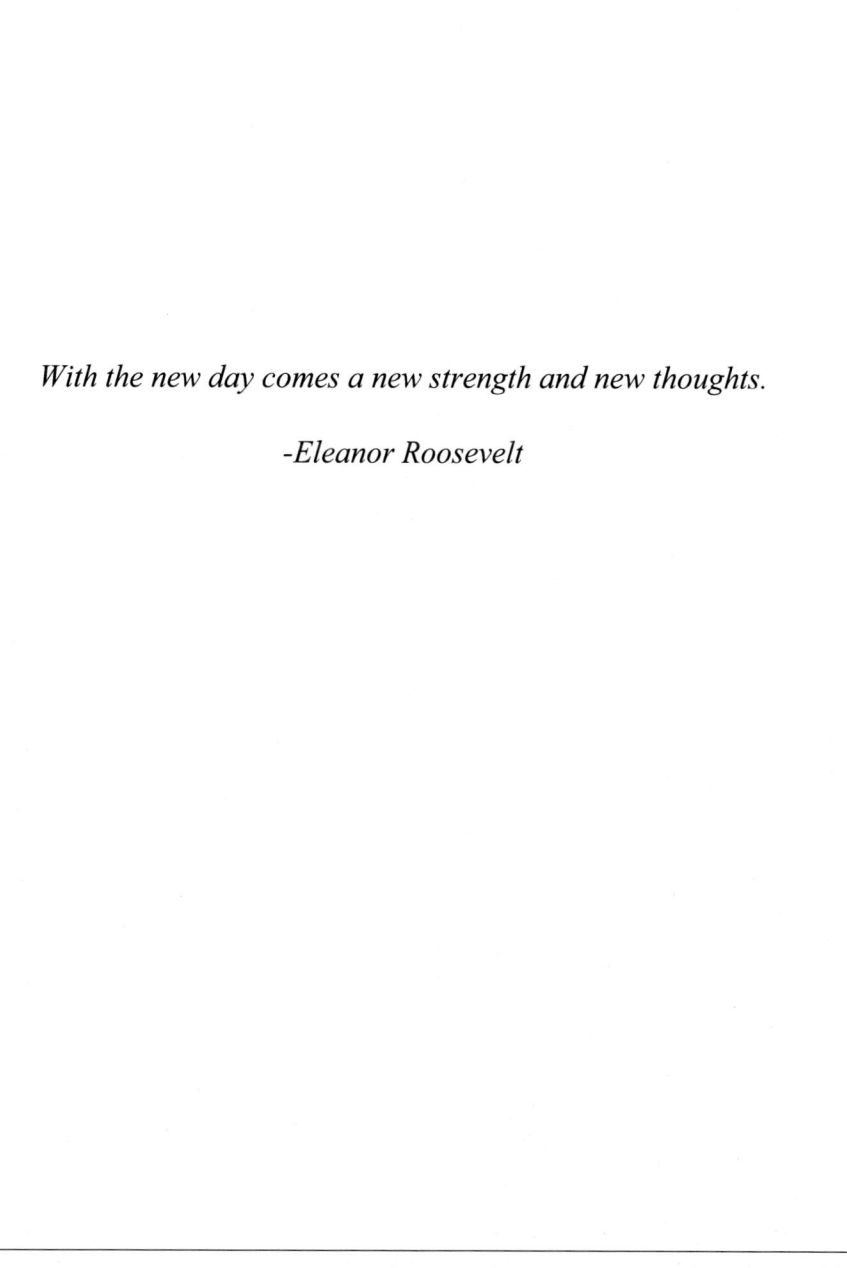

With the new day comes a new strength and new thoughts.

-Eleanor Roosevelt

Dee Dee Callahan Kohler

princemaxrem@gmail.com
774-232-1415
Westborough, MA

I got married later than probably most of my Marian classmates. Had children later. Two boys, Bill born in 1988, John in 1993. My boys are the joy of my life. Finished college later still and by the time I finished a graduate degree in Library Science, I was well into my 50s. I worked as a school librarian in Westborough MA where my husband and I raised our family. For over 20 years, I taught 4th, 5th and 6th graders how to conduct research and introduced them to great literature. I hope I created some lifelong readers along the way. I think Miss Abysalh would have liked that. It's been good. All of it. No regrets.

Those high school years were hard to navigate, so full of angst but I have such fond memories of my time at Marian. Friendship with women has always been a central part of my life. I think that came from my Marian years. I made friends beyond my little neighborhood and I began to understand the wider world around me.

My husband Bill and I retired a couple years back and we are enjoying this time reconnecting with friends and doing some travel. We are looking forward to our first grandchild due in early January 2025!

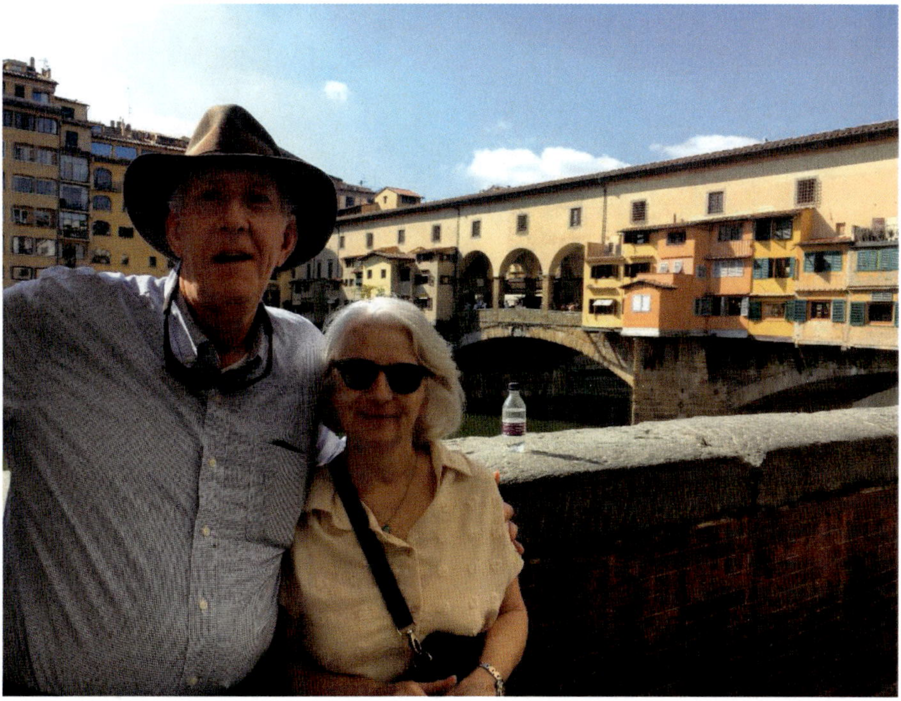

Elizabeth (Betty) Z. Karas Hallinan

ezhxxezh@gmail.com
774-230-6974
Southbridge, MA

I grew up in Holden, MA and presently live in Southbridge, MA. I Attended Worcester State College. I am widowed with no children

Had several career changes during my working years: several positions at Mechanics Bank (then Multibank in Dedham), including Proof Machine, Operator, Overdraft Clerk in Bookkeeping Dept., Transit Supervisor and Data Processing Manager, Admissions at Adcare Hospital, Office Manager at Holden Sanitation, Chef/Owner James Street Restaurant & Dinner Theater.

I liked to travel and have been to France, England, Ireland, Monaco, Canada, many Caribbean Islands, and Mexico. My hobbies include painting and jewelry making.

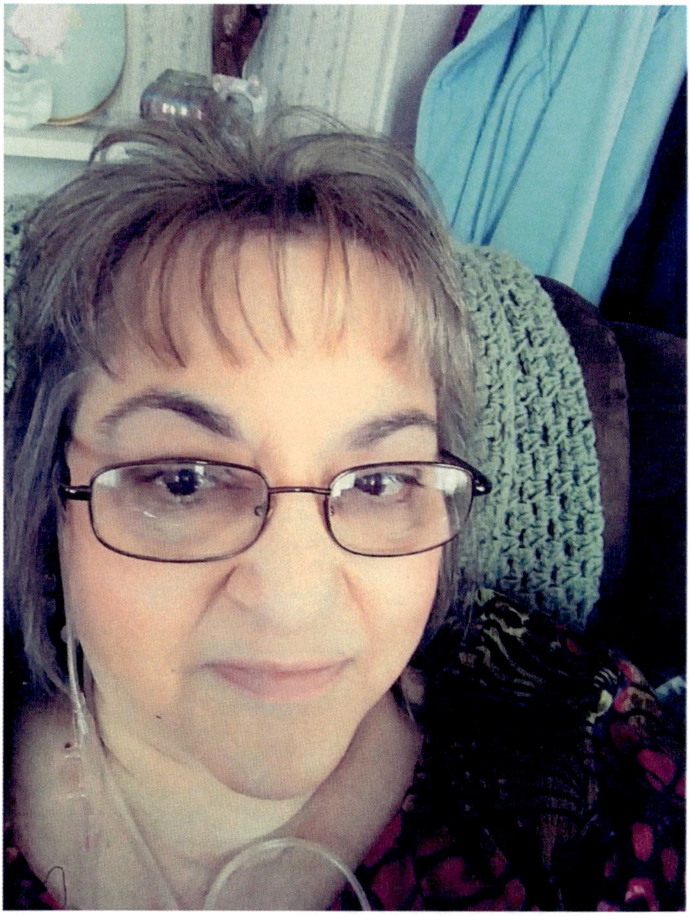

Elizabeth Wright Browning

elizabeth.browning@me.com
508-849-8426
South Dennis, MA

Met my husband the week after we graduated in 1974. Married 44 years, two daughters, five grandchildren (one more on the way!). Recently retired. 44 years working in Healthcare and Healthcare Compliance in health plans and consulting around the country. Living on the Cape in an 1836 sea captain's house which we have been enjoying restoring and renovating.

*All of our dreams can come true,
If we have the courage to pursue them.*
—Walt Disney

Ellen Woods Ryan

ellenryan508@gmail.com
508-954-3827
Portsmouth, RI

Ellen Woods Ryan: Graduated from Emmanuel College in 1978 & was employed at Harvard University in the Planned Giving Program & the Harvard Business School Development Office until 1990.

I married David John Ryan in 1986. He worked in Boston at New England Telephone which ultimately became Verizon Communications. We had our first child Daniel in Boston & moved to Franklin, MA in 1991 due to expanding family. We had 4 children, Dan (1989), Kathleen (1991), Michael (1992), & John (1994). Dan married Tara Fogarty in 2020 (Covid/ family wedding). They now have 2 children: June (2022) & Patrick (2024). Kathleen is currently living & working in London; sons Michael & John live in the Boston area.

Dave & I moved to Portsmouth, RI in 2018 to be near his siblings in the Newport area & bought a boat, enabling us to travel to Martha's Vineyard, Block Island & the towns along the Narragansett Bay. We both have sailing credentials & Dave got his Merchant Mariners license in 2018, allowing him to drive the Newport water taxi for a retirement job.

Dave was diagnosed with bile duct cancer in December 2019 & passed away May 6, 2021. He was able to attend my oldest son's wedding but never met his beautiful grandchildren. He is missed by all who knew him.
I was Therese McKeon Logan's roommate for many years & accompanied Therese & Anne Clancy Nealon to BC Alumni rugby games in the 1980's where they met their husbands. We have stayed close friends since our days at Marian High & still laugh at the crazy antics & memories!

A big "Thank you" to those who organized this reunion! Two of my siblings also graduated from Marian & are anxious to hear about it. See you on September 15th.

Jill McGrath Jones

jill.mcgrathjones@gmail.com
Bowie, MD

My husband, Gary Jones, and I have been married for 32 years. He is a retired Captain of the US Coast Guard, and we currently live in Bowie, MD - outside of Washington DC. The Coast Guard gave us a great life and we lived in DC, New York, London (UK), Cleveland, Honolulu, Boston, Oakland, and then settled back in DC until retirement. During those years, I worked in international aid focusing on disasters and refugee crises for a variety of NGOs.

My work took me to the former Yugoslavia, Indonesia, Pakistan (4 times), Myanmar (Burma) - generally for periods of 4 to 12 months. After so many years of travel, I took a job in DC with the Peace Corps in the office of Global Health and HIV, where I helped train Peace Corps volunteers. After retiring, I volunteered for many years with the Red Cross office at Bethesda Naval /Walter Reed Military hospital aiding wounded soldiers and their families, and other patients. Gary and I moved last year, and now spend most of our time gardening and being retired.

Oh, and one time in Boston, I bumped into Tom Brady, and he and I made out a little in a booth over gin and tonics. He never mentioned that he knew Dee Kohler.

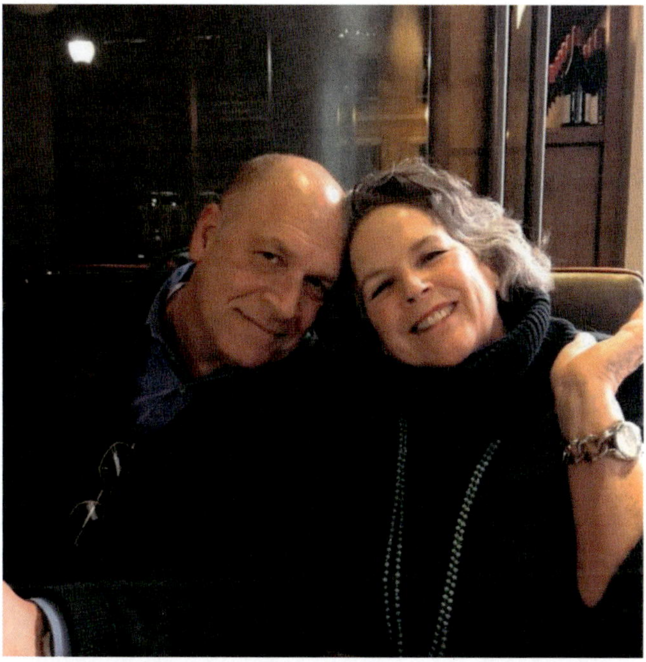

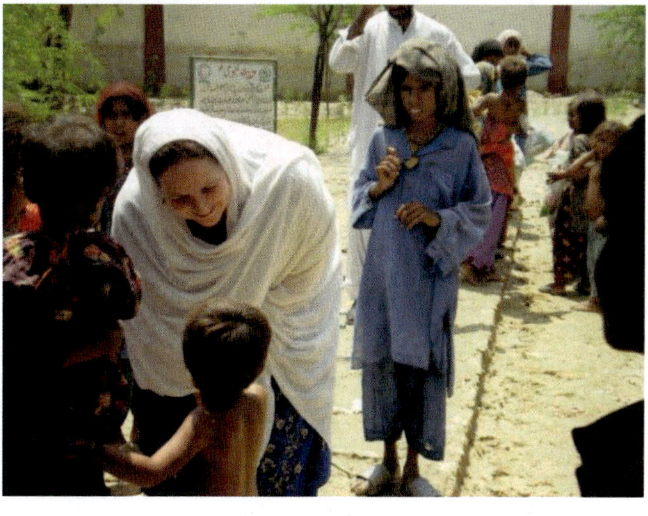

Joan Ladner Mardin

jonmar54@aol.com
508-450-1023
Winter Haven, Florida

I graduated Assumption College in 1978 with degree in mathematics where I played basketball, field hockey, and softball with Rita Castagna as my coach.

I was married in 1983 to George Mardin. I have 3 daughters Lisa, Julie, and Tara and have 5 grandchildren: Riley, Sawyer, Mila, Frankie and Dakota. My husband retired in 2016 and we moved to an over 55 community in Winter Haven, Florida. I have been a bookkeeper since 1978 and continue to work remotely.

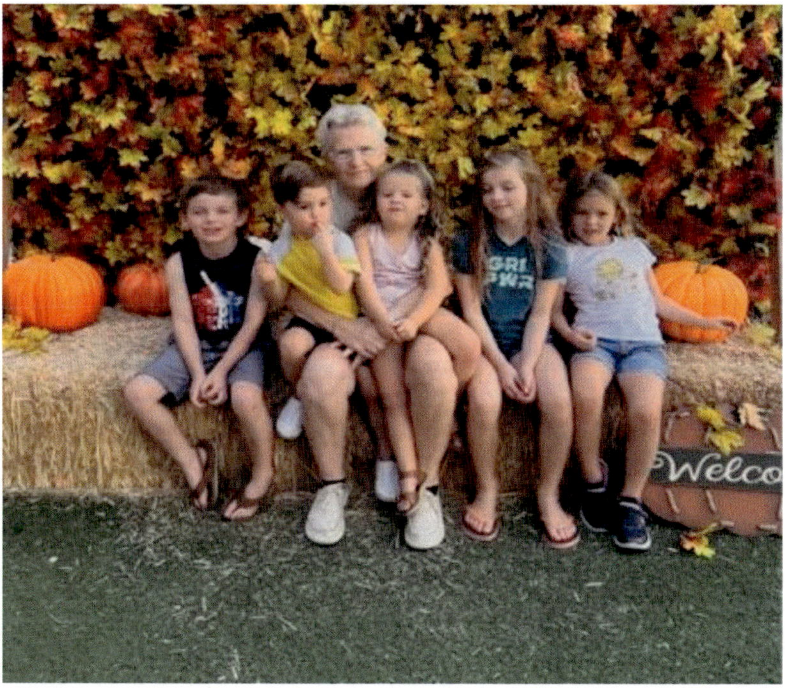
Welco

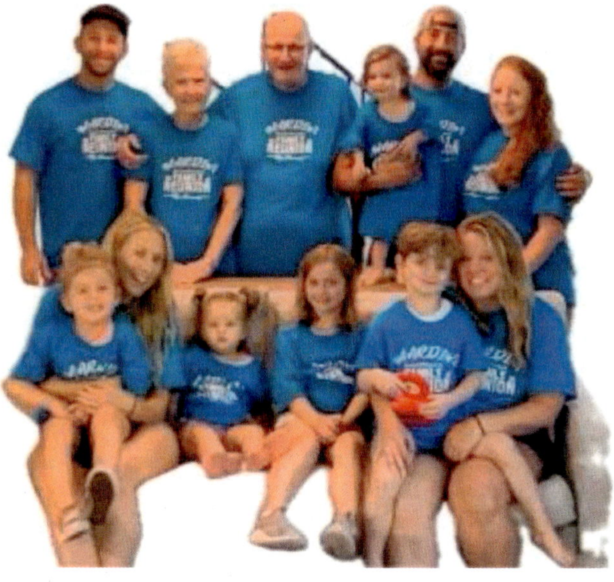

Joan Metivier Bertrand

JlbertrandHR@gmail.com
978-402-8004
Sterling, MA

Following earning my BA in Music I pursued a vocal career and performed in several operatic roles and concerts as a soloist. I had great vocal opportunities including singing under the batons of John Williams and the Boston Pops, and Seiji Ozawa. I also performed locally with several choruses.

After completing my MBA I supported my husband as he completed his medical degree and commitment to the US Navy. I have been married for 45 years, have 2 sons and worked in healthcare for 45 years predominantly in either a VP/Chief of Human Resource role.

I just retired for the 2nd time, but no promises not to go back to work! I served on several non-profit boards to include President of Girls Inc, and Girl Scouts of Central and Western MA. Our fun times are spent on the ballroom floor. My husband and I have competed as a couple and I with my coach in both rhythm and smooth competitions.

We just built our final home on Lake Monomonac in Southern NH. Although my husband has not yet retired we hope to continue following our love for travel. We have visited several countries including Tanzania, Kenya, Egypt, Italy, Baltic countries, Alaska, Greece, Israel, Palestine, Costa Rica and soon to visit Thailand/Vietnam/Saigon.

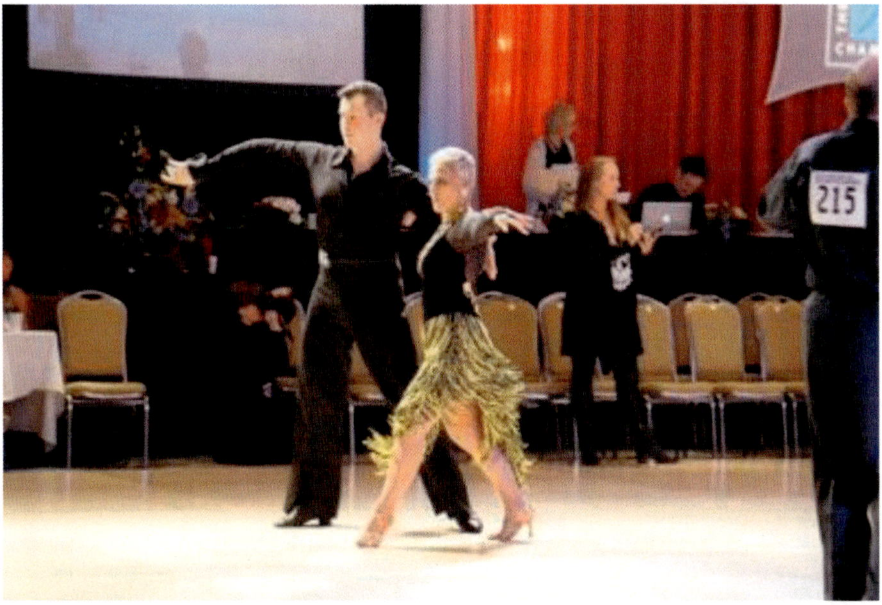
215

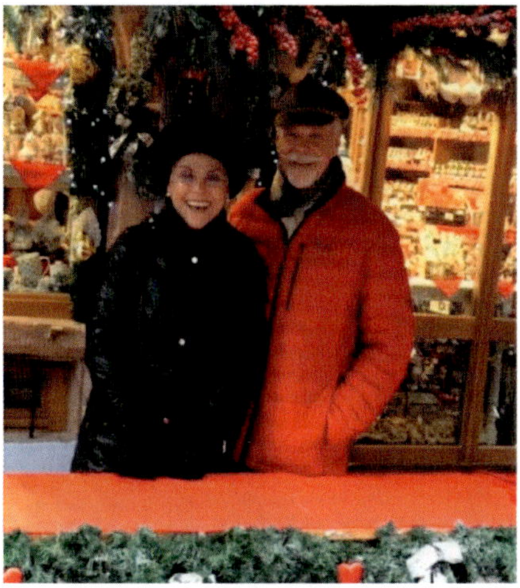

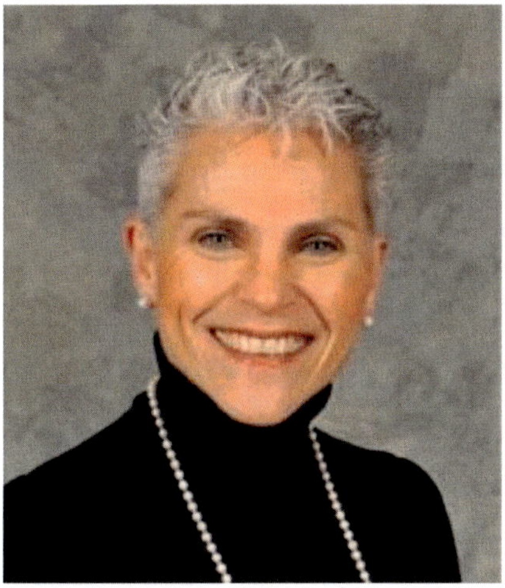

Kathy Hanlon O'Connell

kathyhanlonoconnell@gmail.com
603-313-1428
West Chesterfield, NH

I have been a lifelong learner earning a B.S. from Salem State, Masters from Springfield College and Doctorate later in life. My career was college teaching, a job I absolutely loved. I still teach college level health education courses part time online. I have also been a personal trainer, group fitness instructor, swim instructor, swim coach, and water aerobics instructor. I was with my first husband for 27 years and divorced in 2002. Met my current husband in 2003 and we have been together since then. I have three adult biological children and three adult step children, 12 grandchildren between the ages of 4-14. I have lived in MA., Maine, NH, NY and CT. Currently living in the woods of southwestern NH. I also have a cabin in remote Maine (Rangeley area). I have been a Vegan for the past 7 years.

I love baking, hiking, kayaking, pickleball, card games and coffee. I love chatting with friends from my past and present. When my children were young, I was a quilter, and collected buttons. I served on many town boards when my children were young, such as planning board, conservation, and parks and recreation.

Marian High gave me confidence as a human being and as a female to always strive for excellence and equality. I have so many fond memories, but I remember there was a faculty switch day and I taught religion class for Sister ? Sorry, but I cannot remember her name! I got to be in the faculty lounge for lunch!

I like to think that I have lived a "giving" life. I have been involved in creating a food pantry, food drives, and helping others throughout my life. It is my mission to serve others expecting nothing in return. I've also been a strong advocate for survivors of sexual assault and domestic abuse, knowing first-hand the trauma sexual and domestic abuse can bring. I dream of traveling across the United States in a camper and seeing the many natural wonders of our country.

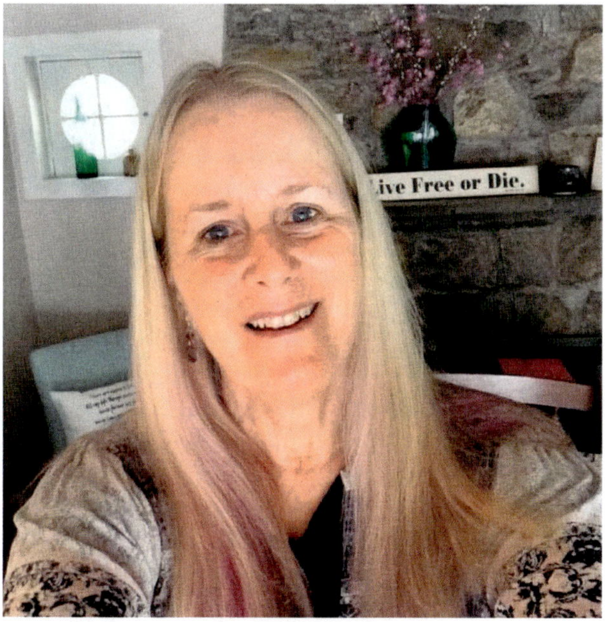
ive Free or Die.

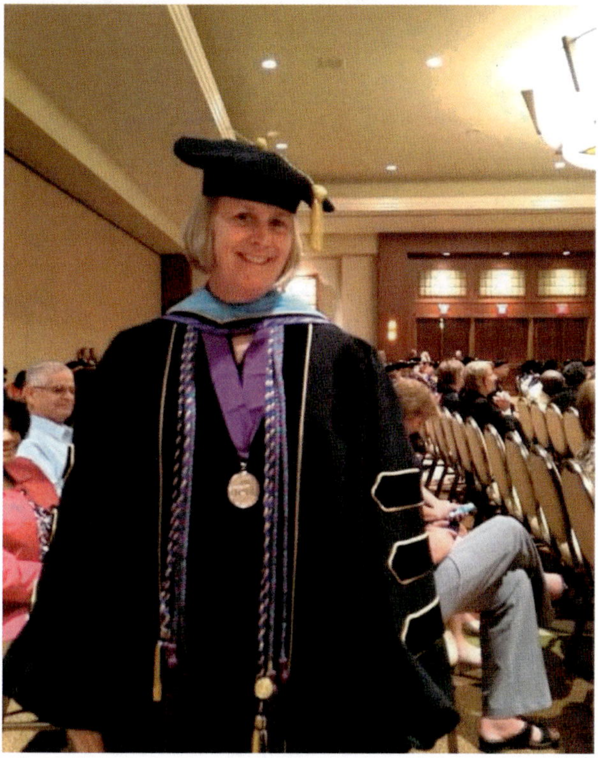

Kathy Hart Harrington

kandhentertainment@charter.net
508-769-2007
Sturbridge, MA

I graduated from Worcester State College and Case Western Reserve University in Cleveland, Ohio in 1979 with a Masters Degree in Speech/Language Pathology.

I married Paul Harrington in 1978. I worked in my field for eight years. We moved to Sturbridge, MA on Big Alum Lake.

I left my field to manage my husband's medical practice, Charlton Family Practice.

I have 3 sons. Ryan, a dentist in Webster, Tim, a singer/songwriter - Tall Heights, and Mikey, a podiatrist at Sturdy Hospital. I have 5 grandchildren, Georgie, Lukey, Gil, Charlie, and Ali.

I continue to work at our medical practice and enjoy my family on the lake!

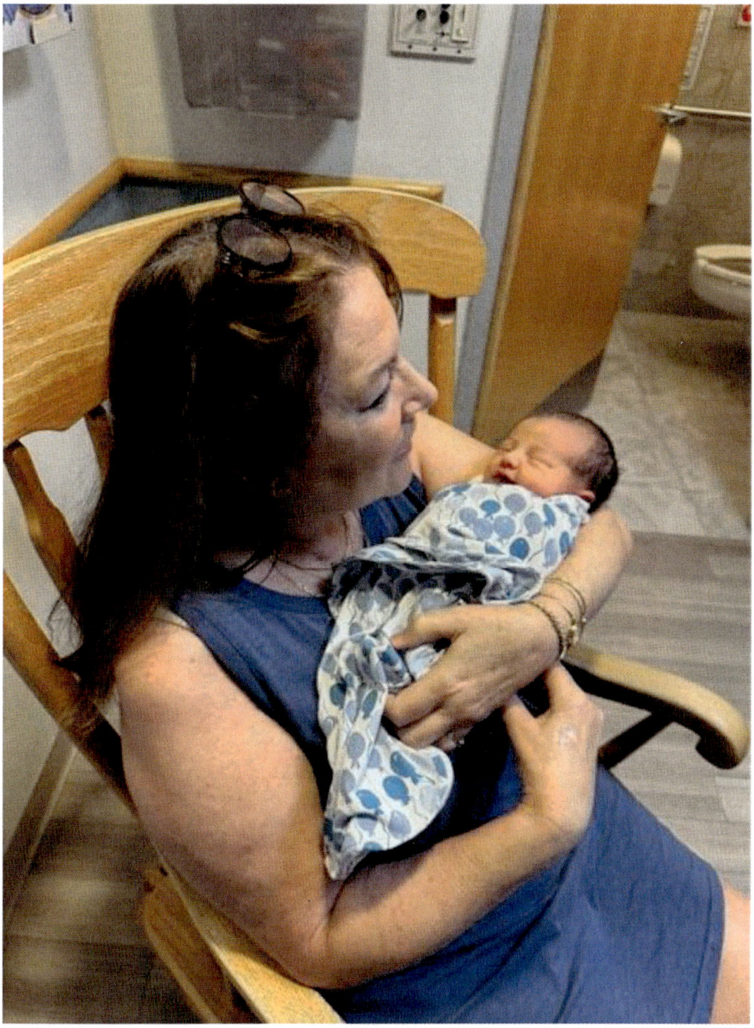

Kathy McMahon Stansky

kmstansky@gmail.com
781-248-2038
Weston, MA

I have a B.S. from the University of Connecticut, Storrs, CT. I attended the Fashion Institute of Technology (FIT) as an adjunct to my undergraduate studies and have a M.Ed from Framingham State University.

I taught in the Worcester Public Schools for a few years prior to working in Manhattan at a Sportswear firm. I married Robert Stansky in 1983 and moved to Boston where I worked as a Marketing Director for an import apparel company.

I live in Weston, MA. Our adult children are Marya, married to Greg Seaman; Matthew who is engaged to Danielle O'Dwyer; Edward and Philip who both live in Boston. Simone Seaman is our 16 mos. old granddaughter whom I enjoy visiting in Brooklyn, NY.

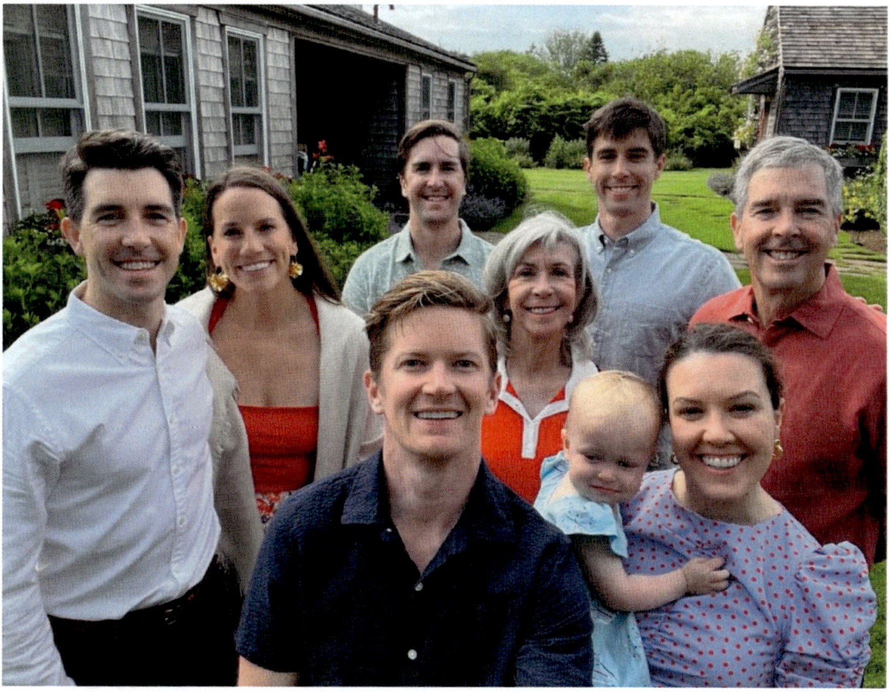

Kathy Naughton Head

wiseowl8455@gmail.com
603-259-6374
White Mountains, NH

Happily married for 43 yrs. Joe and I have a daughter and two grand girls that live two miles away in Littleton, NH.

We moved to the White Mountains in 1992 where I continued my nursing career. I specialized in Oncology and am retired after 40 years in 2016.

I never stopped giving to the community where I visit homebound and bring communion to members of our Catholic Church. My husband has been delivering meals on wheels for 4 yrs.

We travel to a few favorite places each year: Cape Cod and Myrtle Beach. We are enjoying our journey together. Each day is a gift.

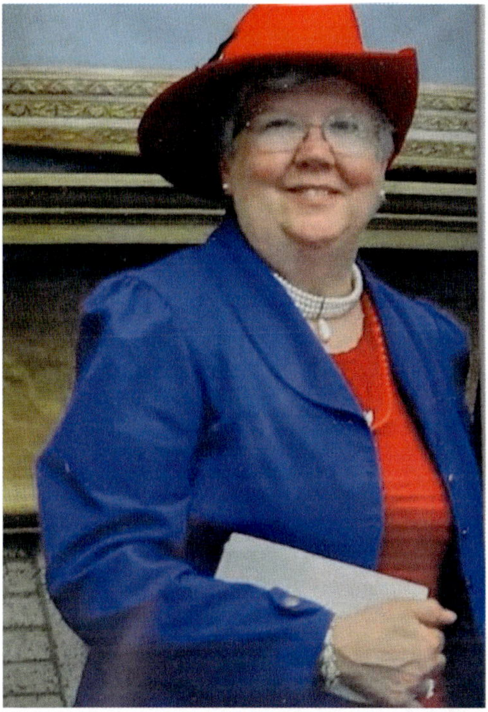

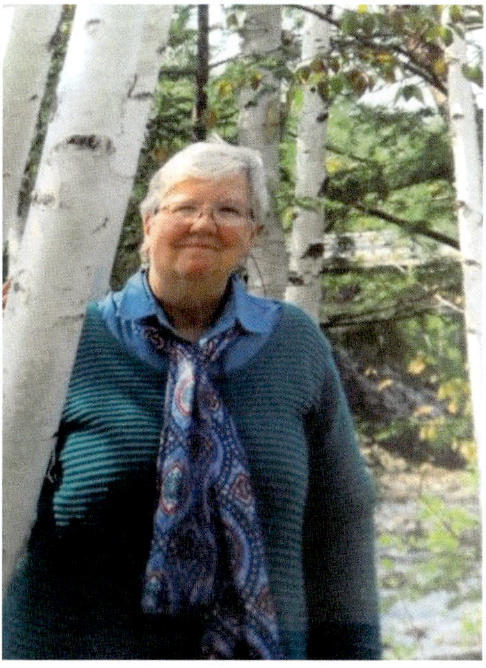

Kathy Robichaud Barnard

kathybma@charter.net
774-312-5621
Worcester, MA

Like everyone else, I cannot believe it's been 50 years. Wow.
I am a lifelong resident of Wormtown - just never left; although I did a bit of traveling.

A twist of something or other led me to an LPN program as a single parent; I later went back to school and got my RN.
Worked a long time in acute care, then in a rehab hospital; wound up in case management for the last part of my career until my health forced me into retirement.

My son has been happily married to my wonderful daughter-in-law for ten years; he'll be turning 48 in October.

I was married to Jeff Barnard for 20 amazing years until he passed away in 2010. I miss him every day.

I keep busy with cross stitch, soap making and my two crazy kitties.
I am unable to attend the reunion, but really enjoy the FB group and seeing what everyone has been up to- not to mention all those photos from the 70s!

Enjoy the reunion! I'll be with you in spirit.

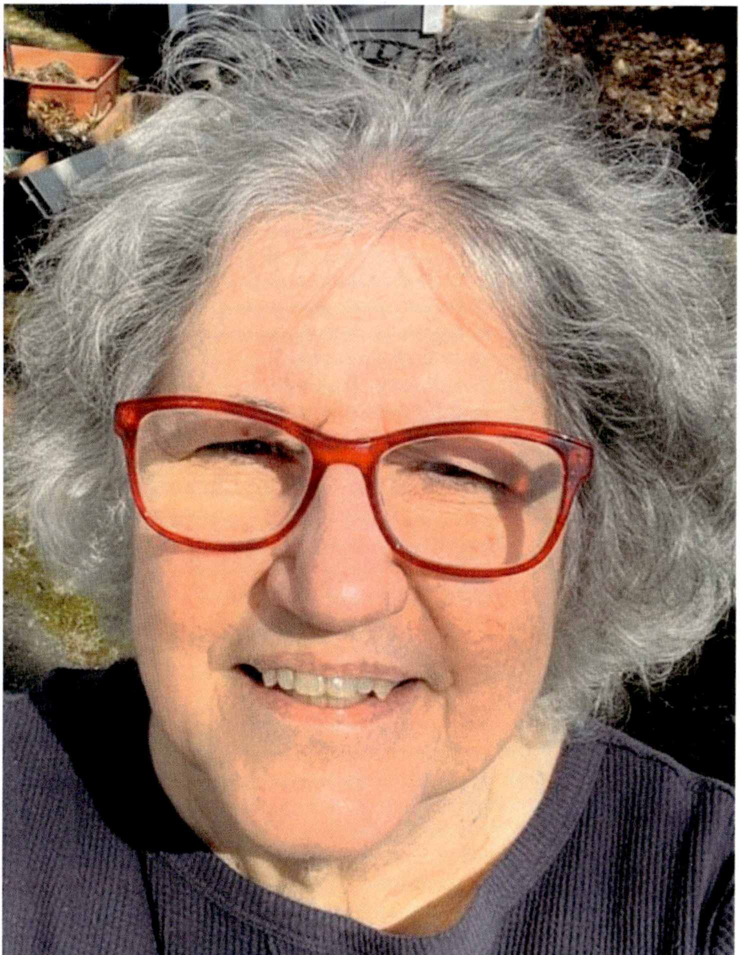

Karen Ritchie Igo

igomom@comcast.net
East Falmouth, MA

I attended Quinsig for a year immediately after high school and graduated from UMass Amherst, moved to Boston, worked at John Hancock and met my husband, Steve, who I have been married to since 1982. I never made it back to Worcester but have lived on the Cape in Falmouth. I have 3 children who are all married with their own children.

After a break from John Hancock to start my family, I worked at HeadStart where I was a teacher and then social worker and coordinator of the Teen Parent Program. I've been involved in non-profits my whole life and currently volunteer in district court as a domestic violence advocate and at the local community service center helping coordinate services with the Greater Boston Food Bank.

I like to golf and I try to travel a few times a year usually choosing one spot in the US and another outside of the country but my favorite vacation is always the annual one with family in Ogunquit, Maine. In addition to my volunteer days every week, I am lucky to spend 2 days with grandchildren and travel to Manhattan every few weeks to visit with the newest addition.

I am looking forward to seeing everyone!

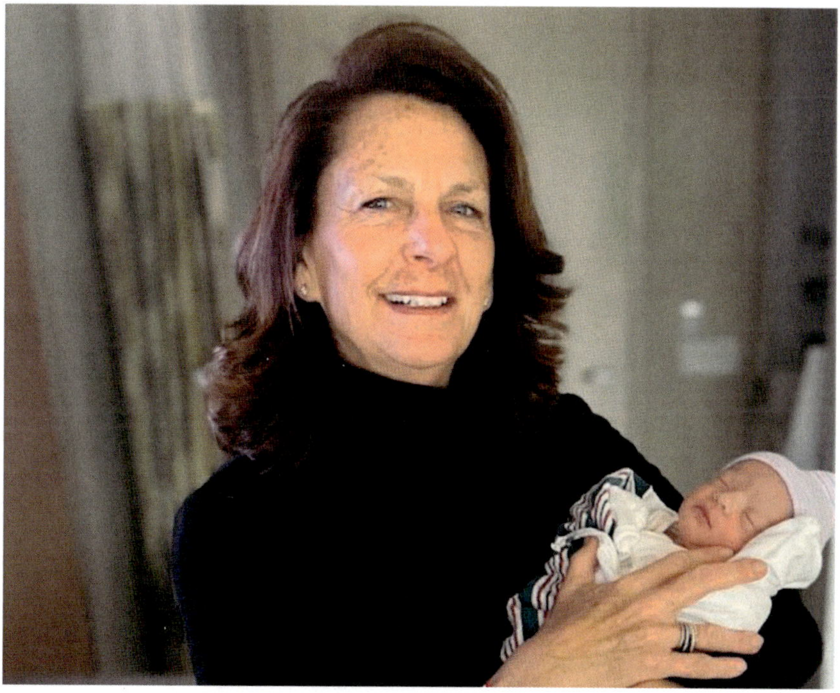

Linda Corriere

508-791-9113 or 508-239-3736
Worcester, MA

January of 1979, I left to join the USAF. I went to San Antonio, TX for my basic training. My first assignment was Carswell AFB Fort Worth, TX. From there I went to Omaha NE then to Ramstein AFB Germany.

I came back to the states and went to Tampa, FL, to Rome, NY, and to my last assignment, Seymour Johnson AFB NC where I retired after 24 years of service.

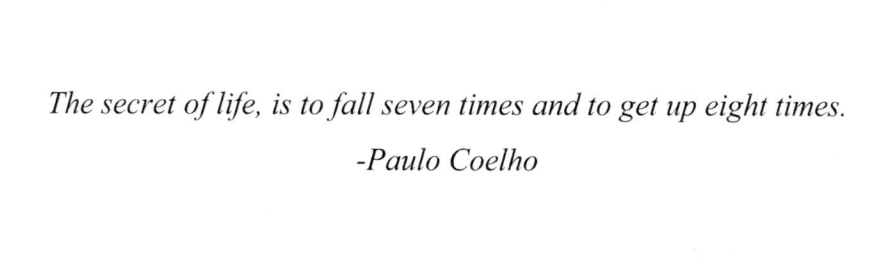

The secret of life, is to fall seven times and to get up eight times.
-Paulo Coelho

Marguerite Savage

savagem119@gmail.com
508-755-3575
Worcester, MA

I dropped the name 'Cookie' a long, long time ago! I was surprised to find it engraved on the cover of my yearbook. My 3 year old niece at the time was very good about reminding people – 'she doesn't want to be called that anymore!'

I graduated from Framingham State University with a BS in Food Science in 1978 and received an MBA from Colorado State University in 1983 – and I never had a career in either field.

I spent 7 weeks biking through Europe in the summer of 1981 – both with a youth hostel group and alone. I remember watching the wedding of Charles and Diana on a TV in the window of a Swiss shop.

I began working for Whole Foods Market in 1993. The closest I will ever come to being a rock star. I worked in many capacities for Whole Foods but finally ended up in Accounting – which I loved!

For part of my career with Whole Foods, I lived and worked in London for 5 years. Loved it! My two cats came with me.

After coming back to the US in 2009, I felt that I needed to 'give back' to the community and became a foster parent. My first placement was an 18 month old girl. I adopted her 2 ½ years later. Her name is Patience and she is now 15 years old. Yikes! (She made her First Communion in the same group with Sheryl Xenos' grandson.)

I now enjoy working for Worcester Academy in the Business Office and hope to retire in 2 years.

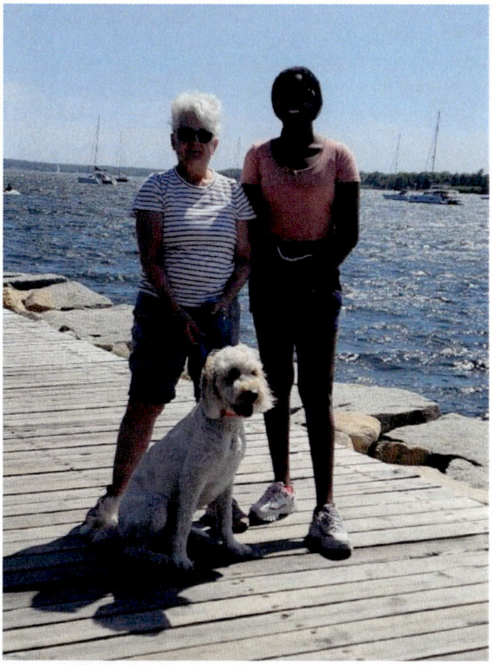

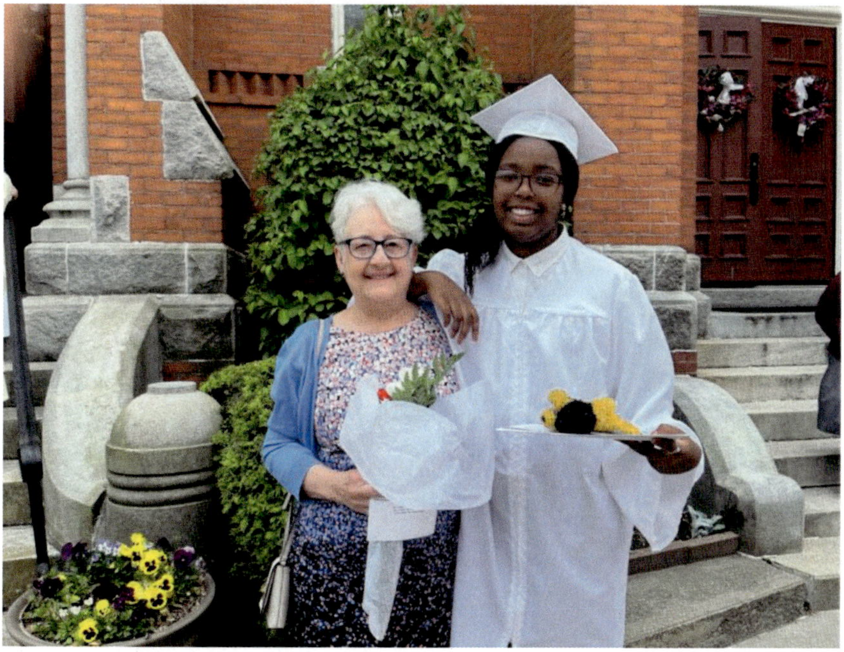

Maryann Harrity Burns

508-868-9630
Charleston, SC

After raising 3 children and having an empty nest, I went to work for 20 years as an elementary school health teacher out in the Fitchburg school system.

Upon retirement, I moved down to Charleston, South Carolina, where I enjoy many daily adventures!

Life in the low-country is super delicious and very historical.

With Deep Life Experience Comes Deep Wisdom.

-Morgan Freeman

Mary Beth Barnicle Rockwell

msingb@hotmail.com
Millbury, MA

Education:
-attended Worcester State College / University
-studied singing, music theory, and piano at Conservatories throughout MA and CT and pursued a career as a vocalist.

Married:
-1976 to Ted Crommett with whom I have 3 children: Katie, age 47, lives in Paxton MA with her husband Jason Lambert. Both are singers and working in outreach and social work. Dennis, 45, a singer/songwriter based in Northampton MA, and married to Kim Logan. Elise, 33 (yup! Oops!) and such a blessing in our lives. She is a singer and marketing consultant in NYC.

Balancing being a "Mom" and "performer" was challenging as I was often out of state for a few days as we moved from MA to CT. In 1995, I was divorced and moved back to Worcester with my 4 year old Elise and 2 children in college. I pursued my career with even more deliberation and success thanks to the Diocese of Worcester, St. Peter-Marian and so many others. Fun times were had when our vocal-dinner/ dance band performed throughout New England.

January of 2001 saw my marriage to "Rob" Rockwell. Life changed dramatically for both of us with the death of our parents in 2004. Life became more about entrepreneurial ventures, fund-raising concerts, and traveling to Ireland. We moved to the coast of Maine for 15 years but returned to central Mass. just before Covid hit. Our home on a pond is complete with our dear yellow Lab, Brook.

I am grateful to be able to share our stories with each other and can't wait to be with everyone at the Reunion.

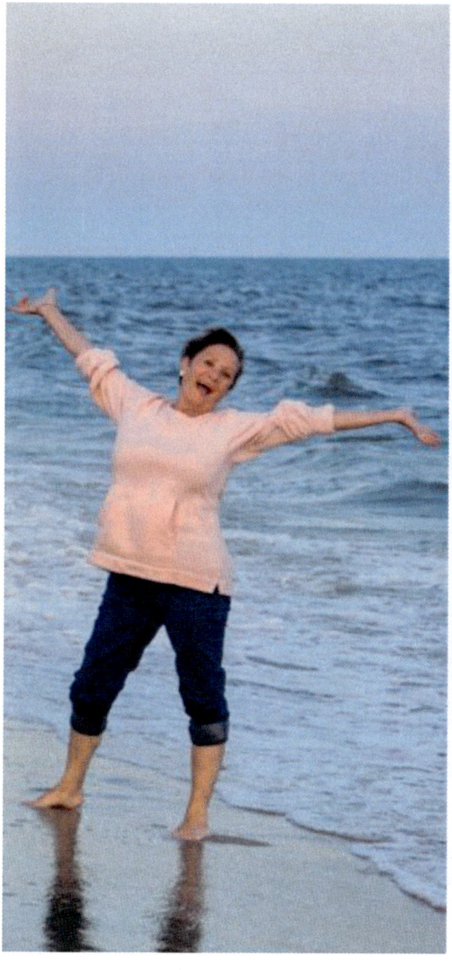

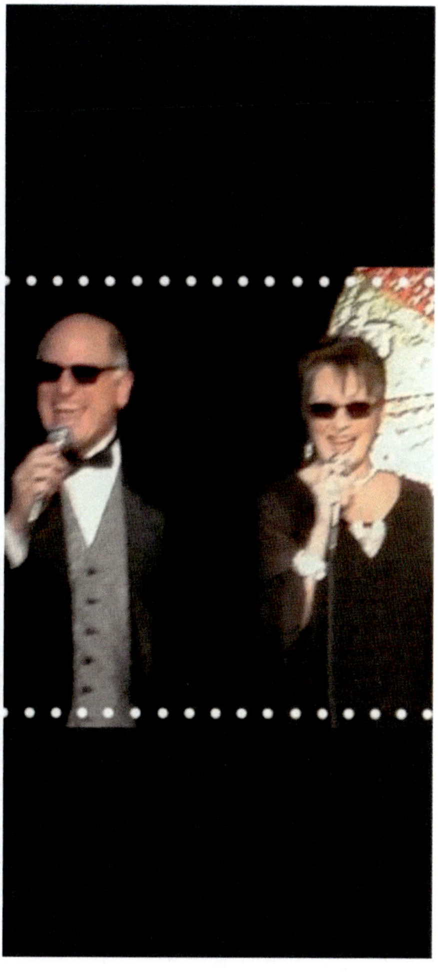

Mary Keenan

maryekeenan56@gmail.com
508-873-3280
Boston, MA

I have been in the eyecare industry for 45+ years. I live and work in Boston. I have three daughters and eight grandchildren. They all reside in Massachusetts.

Mary Murphy Beer

508-736-4449
Holden, MA and Charlestown, NH

Hi, it's Mary Murphy. I have two grown children. My son is married and is a State Trooper (so watch out!). My daughter is married with three girls. They keep Mom and Dad pretty busy. I have been with my companion Bruce for 22 years. We live part-time in Holden and more time in Charlestown, NH. I volunteer at a church working in the thrift store. I love it. I'm the youngest one there. That's all folks!

Maura Conlon

luma56@charter.net
Bolyston, MA

After graduating from Marian, got a degree in Radiology from Quinsigamond Community College. I was an Xray/Cat Scan/Bone Density tech throughout various years at St.V's, Memorial, Fallon, & ending my career at Metrowest Medical Center in Framingham retiring last May.

Have lived in Boylston, Mass for the last 34 years & with my partner/wife for 40 years this year Sept. 14th! Many of those years traveling, our favorites being Mt. Desert Island, Maine, Cape Cod, Midwest, & most recently Iceland. We are soon going to visit my sister in Costa Rica who owns a B&B /Irish pub for the Thanksgiving holiday.

We've spent many years working on our house & yard and also being caregivers here for my younger sister who passed in 2016 & both our moms, most recently mine who just passed in March after a very long healthy 94 years.

I enjoy kayaking & would do it everyday if I could, bicycling, hiking, gardening & birding in these later years (who the hell ever knew what a Baltimore Oriole was) & music. My love for that has never wavered attending many concerts, musicals, plays & Broadway shows since high school. Also I am an avid Patriots fan, especially the years Tom Brady gave us but unfortunately no personal stories with him :)
My years at Marian, although a rough start just moving to Worcester a week before school started & not knowing a soul, were a wonderful part of my life. It was actually an advantage not being a part of any of the cliques coming from the junior highs, Harrington Way, Tatnuck, Newton & Webster Squares enabling me to make friends with almost everybody. I still have contact with a few till this day.

Marian instilled in me great morals in how to treat others continuing on how I was raised. My pride & love of my parents, siblings & extended families throughout the years has brought me immeasurable happiness & also strength getting thru some tragic losses along the way.

Retirement has been wonderful, so much time to enjoy more travels & the opportunity to have taken care of my mom who was also my best bud. I look forward to what the rest of the future holds.

I am very excited for the reunion & ABSOLUTELY cannot believe it has been 50 years.

Maureen Corrigan Rourke

Moern@comcast.net
Naples, FL

I graduated from St. Anselm's college BSN in nursing. Just retired from Lahey Clinic after 35 years there in critical care nursing. I raised three children, including two boys and a girl in Nashua New Hampshire. Then sold the house two years ago after COVID.

Now, I divide my time between Cape Cod where my oldest lives with one daughter and then off to Florida where my middle son lives with his three kids. My youngest daughter is a teacher in Burlington Vermont.

We are so lucky to have our health to travel!!!

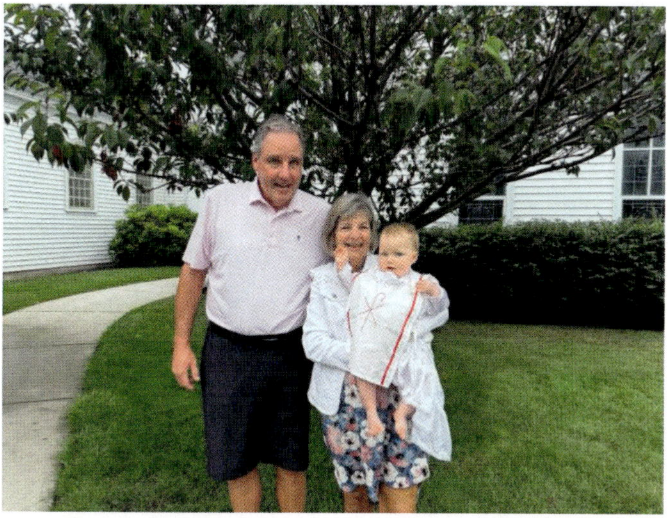

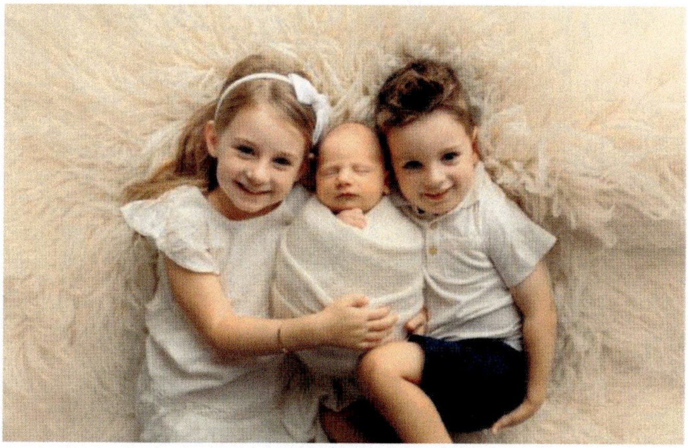

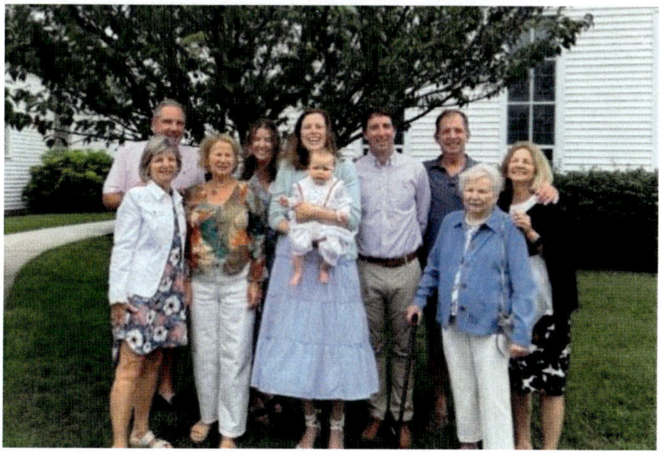

Maureen Errede Bumann

mbumann@comcast.net
978-602-5686
Lunenburg, MA

Graduated from Worcester State College with a BS in Business Administration which lead me to a career in Human Resources. My last 23 years was spent working in Talent Acquisition recruiting engineers for Raytheon until I recently retired.

Married to my husband Eric for 29 years, we reside in Lunenburg MA with our German Shorthair pointer, Viper. Our son, Joseph, relocated to Oregon with his wife, Poonam, after they were married in 2019. He has one step son named Jai. Joseph works as a Senior User Experience Designer after graduating with his MS degree.

Eric and I love to travel both domestically and internationally. We've been fortunate to visit Hawaii, Alaska, St. John, St. Thomas, Bahamas, Aruba, Mexico, France and, most recently, Italy(my favorite). We also love hiking with Viper.

A favorite hobby of mine is exercising which includes, strength training, swimming, pilates, yoga and walking. Life is good!!

75

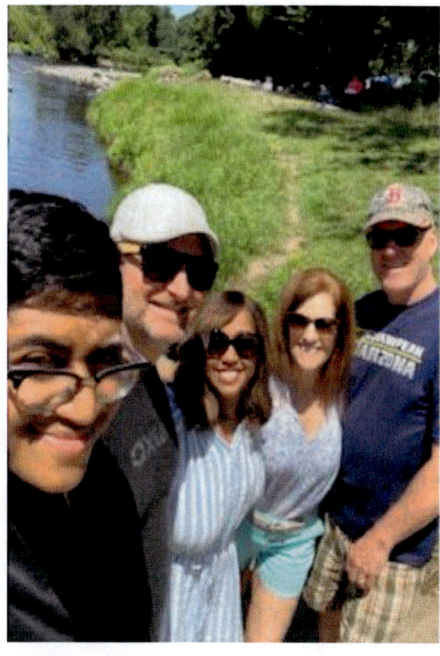

Michelle O'Neil Elliott

Chelelly44@yahoo.com
508-479-3290
Auburn, MA

After graduating from Marian, I received an AA degree from Quinsig. I worked as a bank teller for a short time, got married in 1978, moved to Auburn, then took a position as an ophthalmic assistant at Fallon Clinic. I cut my schedule to part time after my daughter Deanna was born, but after my son Timothy was born, I ran a home daycare.

I returned to Quinsig when Tim was two to become an RN, but switched my major to Occupational Therapy after learning more about it. I worked as an OT assistant for a school collaborative in N. Oxford, then in a nursing center in Webster, while transferring to a BS program for OT at Worcester State. I then worked for the Worcester VNA, before taking a therapist position in two Nursing/Rehab Centers in Marlboro, and worked for 15 years in each of them, 5 of those years as a Rehab Director.

I have been married for 46 yrs and we both retired in 2022. We have 4 grandsons from 9 yrs to almost 3, one bonus granddaughter (18) and a grandson (16). Deanna and her family live in NH, Tim lived in CA for 9 yrs, (so we vacationed there in the spring) but his family moved back to MA in 2018. My husband and I have a time-share in FL and have a summer home on the Cape. We are enjoying retirement and being able to spend more time with our families, grandkids and dear friends. I'm looking forward to our reunion!

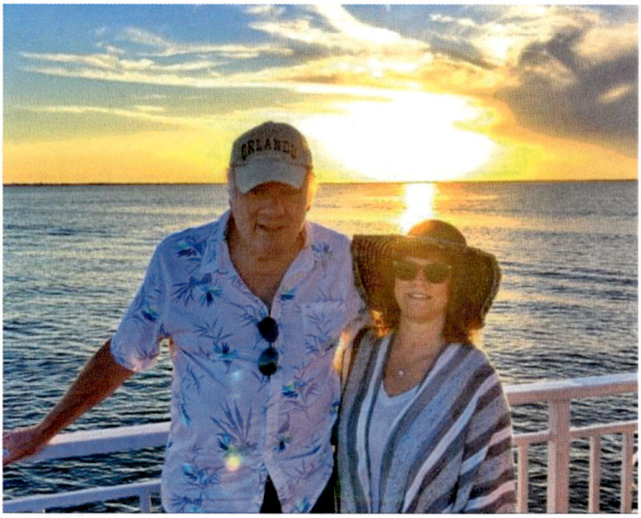
ORLANDO

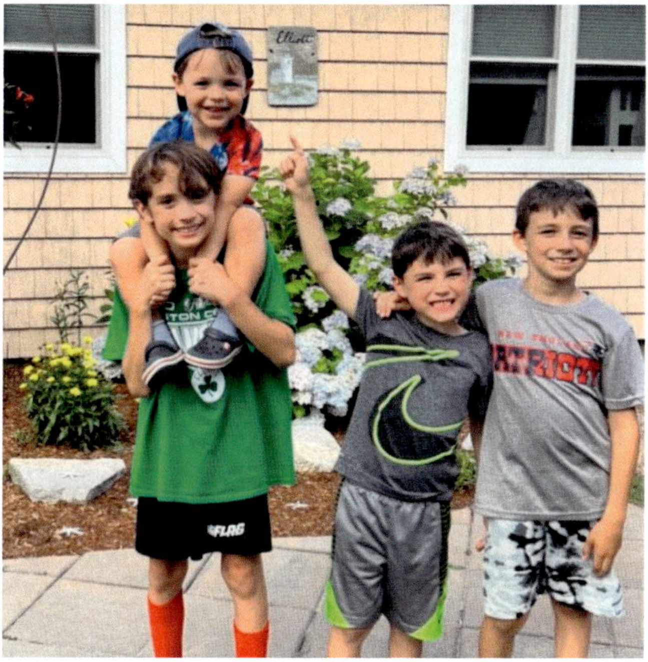
Elliott

Nancy Gardiner Thibault

nancy.j.thibault@gmail.com
508-523-4993
Shrewsbury, MA

I earned a degree in Special Education and Elementary Education from Boston College. After graduation, I spent years teaching while my three daughters were young. Later I redirected my career toward the business sector and worked for a subsidiary of Exxon Enterprises and later at Staples Corporation.

In later years, I felt drawn to the nonprofit sector, and joined Easter Seals MA, contributing to the mission of empowering individuals with disabilities. Presently, I work at Rainbow Child Development Center, a small nonprofit in Worcester. My role involves securing grants to fund enrichment programs for underserved children. This position allows me to combine my background in education with my business experience.

I'm blessed with a fulfilling family life having three grown daughters and five grandchildren who bring joy and laughter to our lives. My husband and I cherish the time spent with our fun-loving grandkiddos creating lasting memories!

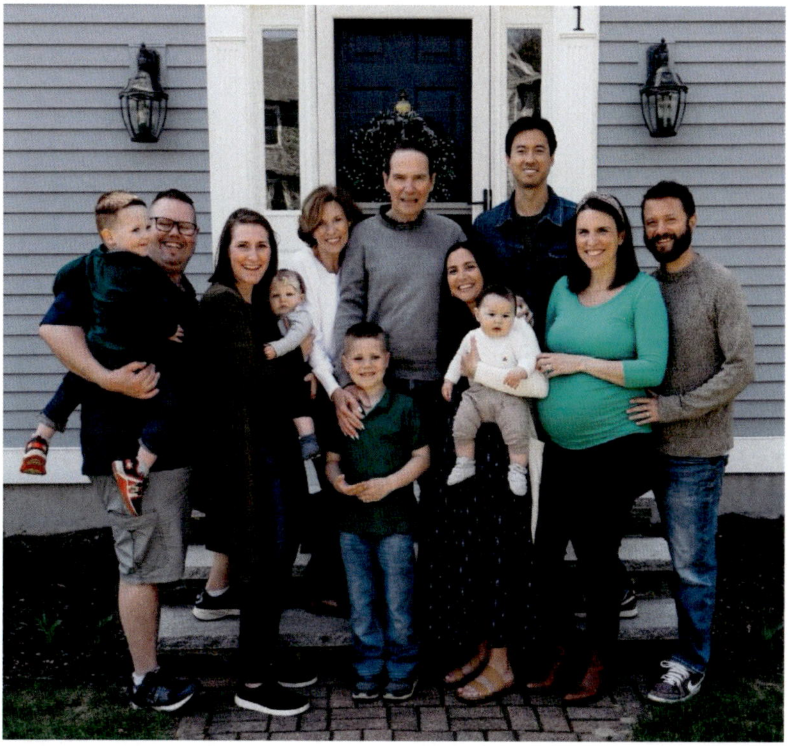
1

Noreen LaHair Davieau

noreenmd@msn.com
Worcester, MA

I married Raymond Davieau Nov. 12,1977. We have 2 children, Erin age 41 and Michael age 39. Both kids are married and between them we have 5 grandchildren.

I retired from the communications department for the city of Worcester in 2017. My husband retired from the post office in 2020. We travel and cruise a lot. Also babysit the grandchildren a lot!

We have a trailer in Rhode Island where we spend most weekends from April to end of October. And...we still live in Worcester!

Not too exciting but we are enjoying life!

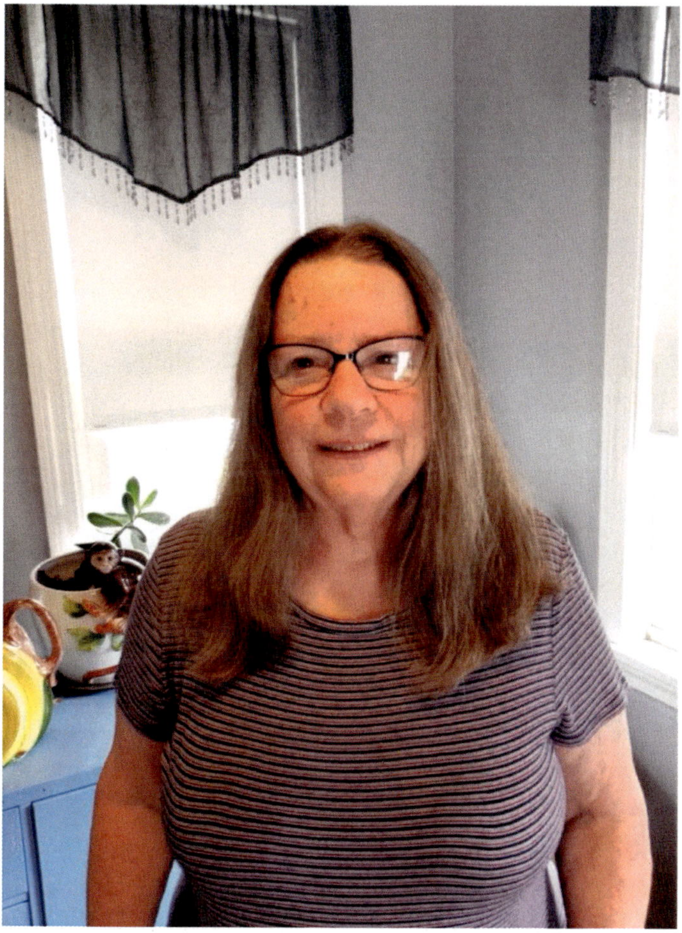

Patty Boulay Cook

trish82633@yahoo.com
303-808-9439
Douglas, WY

It is hard to believe that 50 years has gone by. After High School Graduation, I decided not to go to college for a year. I truly believed that I needed to get a job, go out in the world, and pay my dues. So I moved out of my parents' house (much to their dismay and without their blessings), rented an apartment in a 3 decker on May Street with my sister, and I took a job at Mechanics Bank as a "Return-Items Teller". Essentially, I bounced people's checks for a living. I hitch-hiked back and forth to work every day, washed clothes at a local laundry mat, confiscated toilet paper from a local bar, and saved my wages of $1.88 per hour to attend college in Colorado the following year.

Two days before Christmas, my sister and I set our alarm to 3:00 AM and stealthily proceeded to a nearby Christmas Tree Lot to liberate a Charlie Brown tree and drag it home to our apartment. Of course, I was the one who had to scale the 8 foot fence in 10 degree, chill-to-the-bone weather and drag the heavy tree over to the edge of the lot. I will never forgive my sister for insisting on a second choice of tree because she didn't like the first one I chose. I muttered something about beggars not being choosers. I left an envelope with $5 inside the screen door of the tree lot's office and we scooted back home. All did work out in the end and we did not spend the Holidays in custody. The next day, we invited our friends over to decorate the tree with strings of popcorn, colorful paper rings and homemade ornaments. And there was, after all, Christmas punch with alcohol involved.

For weekly entertainment, I volunteered at the Worcester Foothills Theatre in the old Denholm's building. Of course, I dated a few of the actors that year and was invited to many after show parties. I would walk back and forth through downtown to the Theatre and became a familiar friend to several of the "street girls" there. "Hi, Babette! Hi, Charlotte!" was a common greeting from me on the weekend evenings. Actually, the "girls" would kind of watch out for me and advise me not to walk too close to the alleys where I could be grabbed or too close to the street where the police cars patrolled. Charlotte gave me a spray can of mace to carry with me. As it turned out, there were sisters living on the 3rd floor of our 3 Decker and they were in the "business" too, and the stories they would tell us-were just hysterical! Oh, the joys of being young, poor, and single in the BIG CITY!

Come summer of 1975, I waved good-bye to Mechanics Bank and good-bye to Worcester. I made amends with my parents and hit the trail to Colorado with my Fuji 10 speed bicycle. I actually took the Amtrak to Charleston, WV, arrived at 4:00 AM, unpacked my bike and pedaled off in the early dawn light into a new life! My travel across the country took about two months and was complete with many adventures. At night, I slept in state parks in a pup tent or sometimes on a back porch of those I met or (very often) in local cemeteries because the grass was well groomed, it was very quiet, and no one bothered me! Perhaps, it was my humorous Edward Gorey sense of the macabre that lead me to the cemeteries or just my sense of being poor and practical. I will never forget Jesse Sloan—a 15 year old--in Kentucky who I met while riding through Rush County one day and he invited me to his mom's house to stay the night. Mrs. Sloan had 9 children who lived in a mountain, two bedroom cabin. There were many shared beds. Her older son distilled and sold their own brand of alcohol to many county patrons. Needless to say, I tried my first and only taste of authentic Moonshine that night!

Eventually, I made it to Colorado and pedaled that last few mountain miles into Leadville—former home of the Unsinkable Molly Brown, The Silver Dollar Saloon (which Emmylou Harris wrote about) and Colorado Mountain College where I was to begin my college career. For the first month, I didn't have a place to stay so I would sneak into the college library at closing and sleep on their couches at night. It was actually very decent accommodations. The library had a bathroom, shower, TV, snack machine, and comfortable heat—and all for free (more or less.)

Later that summer, I saw a flyer posting of a beautiful A-Frame cabin that was renting out the basement area to a college student. I went around the campus and took down ALL the flyers then contacted the owner to rent out the place. The owner could never figure out why I was the only person to respond to his flyer. I told him that my mother didn't raise no fool and my father taught me to go after what I wanted in life. This is how I met my future husband. Mark and I were married for many years!

Mark and I were married in 1978 in Estes Park, Colorado (the eastern gateway to Rocky Mountain Nat'l Park) and home of the Stanley Hotel which was Stephen King's inspiration for his book "The Shining". And, yes, they still host ghost tours at the Stanley and I still possess my Stanley Hotel Room key for #217! (Redrum, Redrum! You can still hear whispered in the wind during December storms!) Mark was a ranger at Rocky Mountain Nat'l Park and I began my education career as a school bus driver and substitute teacher.

When you are employed by the Park Service, you move a lot but live in some of the most beautiful, scenic sites in the country. We traveled, lived and worked at Glen Canyon Nat'l Recreation Area (UT), Devils Tower Nat'l Monument (WY-think "Close Encounters of a Third Kind") and Bandelier Nat'l Monument (NM-think Los Alamos and Oppenheimer). Along the way, we had two daughters, Brie and Shawna, who became quite use to packing and unpacking, as well as starting in new schools and making new friends.

We built a log cabin in the mountains near Colorado's Crested Butte Ski Resort. We lived on the Navajo Indian Reservation (NM) where I taught elementary students. I received my Bachelor's, Master's, and Ph.D. My education career covered: being a teacher, principal, school psychologist, curriculum director, director of special education, and

Assistant Superintendent. I worked in a one-room school house, private school for the gifted, rural school districts, large urban districts, and mountain districts. (One time, I was interviewing for a job in WY and the HR manager asked me "What do you like to be called?" Never thinking that I would be offered this job and completely out of thin air, I said with a big smile "Call me Trish!" I got the job---hmmmm!)

Mark passed away in 2022 after a long battle with cancer and my girls have grown into beautiful remarkable, confident women--embodying strength and a spirit of adventure that has taken them around the world. Brie lives in Denver, Colorado and runs a tech company. I am always amazed at her knowledge of the tech world. She is responsible for helping me get this Biography Book printed and published. Shawna (EMT and CNA) lives with me in Douglas, WY and has a highly active 3 year old daughter, Bliss Rose, whose playful spirit and boundless imagination make each day a joy! Travel has been a part of our lives. We have attended a Summer Olympics in London, Winter Olympics in Sochi, cruised the Caribbean, traveled to Hawaii, Ireland, France, Iceland and many more countries.

In many ways, I feel that I have come full circle with attendance at our 50th Marian Reunion. Marian was not just a school but a cornerstone of my life, shaping who I am today. Marian taught me the importance of community, the power of resilience, and the strength that comes from faith. The friendships, the challenges, the laughter and the memories have all contributed to my personal journey. I am grateful to my high school companions, my teachers, and those with the vision to open and lead the school. To all: May the road always rise to meet you…may the wind be always at your back…and until we meet again, may God hold you in the palm of His hand!

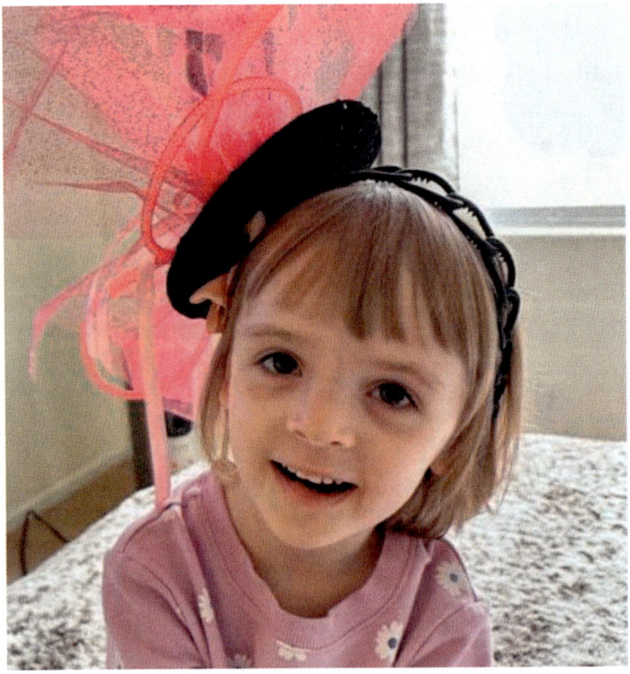

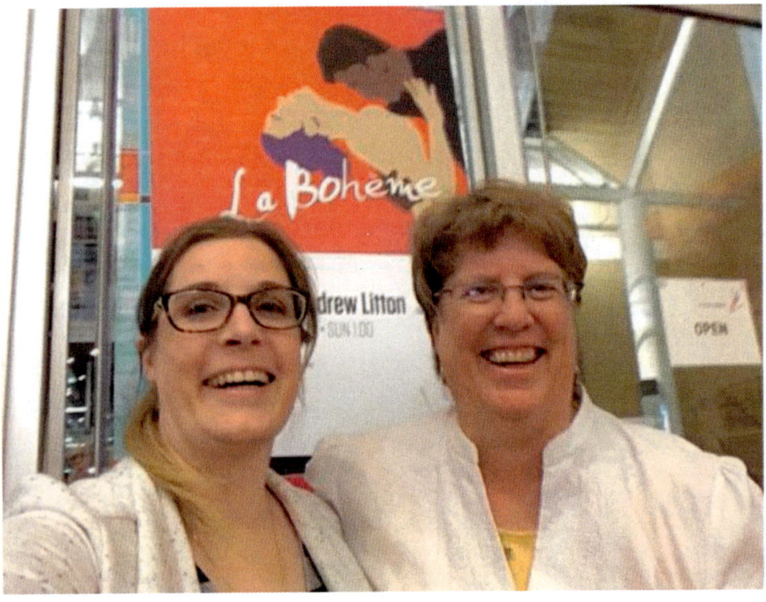
La Boheme
OPEN

The Best Artists Know What To Leave Out.

-Charles de Lint

Paula Garrepy Matthew

508-277-6583
Holden, MA

I worked in healthcare administrative side my entire work life. Billing, scheduling, patient liaison and advocate, front end Office Manager....16 years in several departments at Fallon Clinic/ Reliant Medical Group. My three kids at my son Jeffrey's Army graduation. Laura, Jeff, Jason. That is me....proud Mom wearing her Army Mom jacket. These are my kids and spouses/partners with some of my grand puppies in our favorite place.....Maine.

I have enjoyed horses and have ridden since Jr High. Owned my own horse until 10 years ago....volunteered at the barn working and helping to rehabilitate horses rescued from auctions. Presently part of a Photography Group in Holden trying to increase my ability to capture beautiful scenes and preserve memories. Have recently become part of the Alzheimer Awareness committee, volunteering wherever needed. Alzheimer's claimed my beloved Dad and I hope to help educate, assist and support any families or caregivers struggling with this cruel disease. I still volunteer whenever called upon with two dog rescue groups to help dogs in transition until they find their new fur-ever homes.

Marian taught me to believe in myself, to fight for the underdog, stand firm in my belief to make the world a better place for all humans and all furbabies. It introduced me to my still BEST friend.....Kathy Hanlon who helped teach me to play guitar and sing at folk Masses. Still a member of St George's Parish where I was brought up. I no longer play at Masses (just for myself and my dogs). Maine and the ocean, my strong and giving children, my unconditionally loving dogs will forever make me smile and bring peace to my heart.

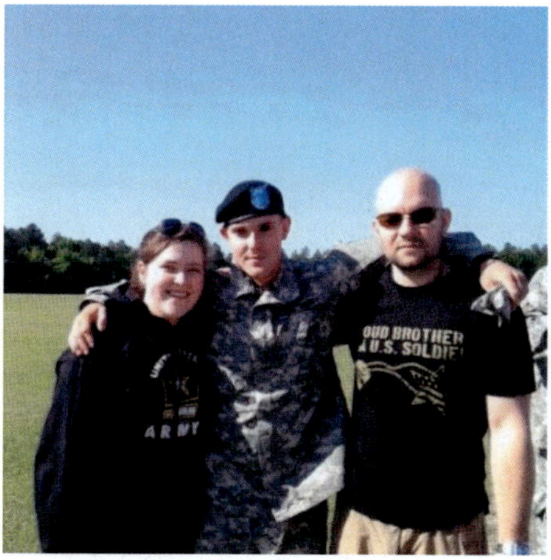
ARMY
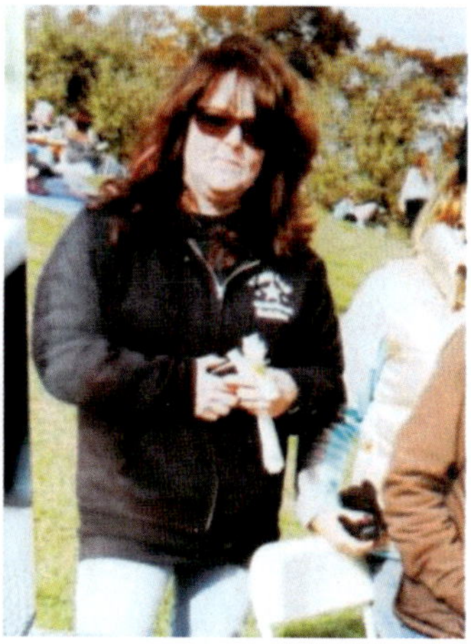
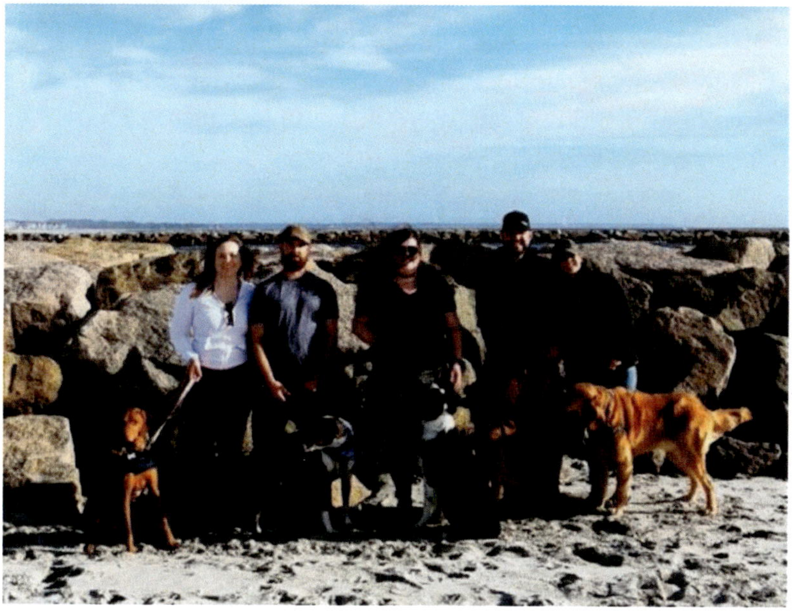

Rosemary Deedy Goodman

rhodeedy@yahoo.com
508-527-8553
Dennis Port, MA and Erie, CO

I am a retired nurse living on Cape Cod and in Colorado. I have been married for 36 years to my husband David, a now retired dentist. We have 2 children living in Colorado and 2 beautiful granddaughters. I worked for years at Worcester City Hospital and Worcester Memorial Hospital then Blue Cross Blue Shield of MA. I retired as the Appeals Specialist for the company. I also was a substitute school nurse for the town of Foxboro and summer camps. I now spend my time helping watch my 2 grandchildren and traveling with my husband.

Sorry I am unable to attend the reunion. I will be back in Colorado. Have fun!

If you have knowledge, let others light their candles from it.

- Margaret Fuller

Sally Nawn Hartmann

Shart15861@aol.com
508-776-5432
Forestdale, MA

My husband Peter and I have been married 45 years! I have three children Kelley, Scott and Peter and four grandchildren Copley, Melody and Dylan (granddaughters) and Peter (grandson). Three grand-dogs named Kramer (Scott's retired Seeing Eye Guide Black Lab) Dylan Scott's current (Seeing Eye Guide Black Lab) and Coco Granddaughters Golden Retriever.

After graduating from Merrimack College I worked in the administrative field and the last twenty years at Joint Base Cape Cod Environmental. I retired in 2021 during Covid.

I really enjoy yoga, travel, and the beach on Cape Cod where we have lived since 1993.

Marian influenced me intellectually and socially. The best friends forever!

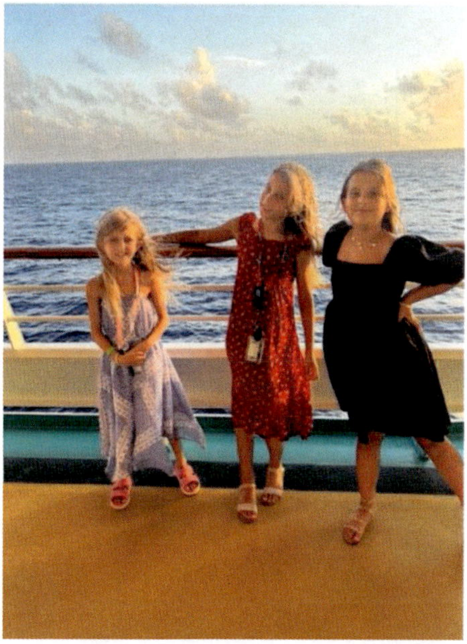

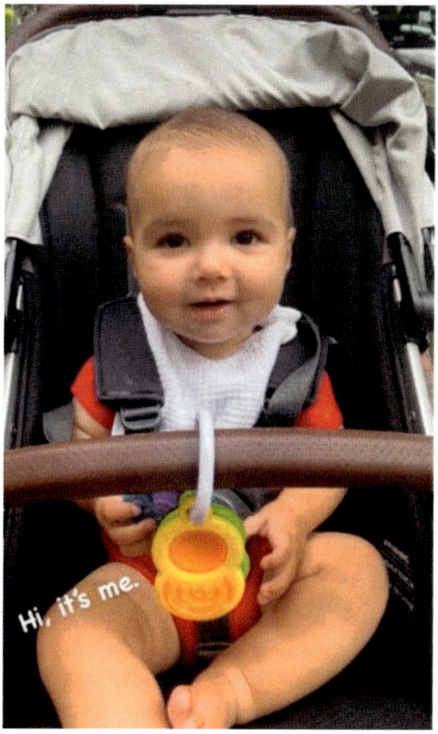
Hi, it's me.

Stephanie (Cullen) Abisla

sabisla1@verizon.net
508-989-9622
Milford, MA

Family – I am one of 4 girls, and I was fortunate to grow up in an extended family. Paternal grandfather lived a mile away (passed in 1978). Maternal grandmother lived next door (passed in 1986). Dad passed in 1991. I married in 1992. I have no children but have a close relationship with my nieces and nephews (all 12, from both sides). Mom passed in 2018.

Education - After Marian, I went to Assumption College for my undergraduate in Biology. I thought of going into Medical Technology, even taking the Civil Service Test. Took the "junior" version which turned out to be all about the equipment while "senior" included the science and theory. I passed anyway! I decided that being in a lab all day was not what I wanted so I returned to Assumption and earned a Masters in Education. One of best decisions and with a great Advisor!!! Got lifetime certification in 6 areas of teaching (Grades 7-12: Biology, Chemistry, General Science, Mathematics, Social Studies, and English)

Occupation - Began teaching and taught in a variety of settings…Diocesan, vocational, regional schools followed by assuming a department chair at Fisher college. While at the college, I earned a Master of Mathematics at WPI then transitioned into teaching within a business setting for a number of years – getting promoted from technical staffing to management, but my heart was still in teaching….. I returned to teaching in 2003 at the Middle School level (primarily $7^{th}/8^{th}$ grade) and remained through Covid – remote, hybrid, and back to classroom. Family stresses (Mom's passing and Mother-in-law transitioning into Assisted Living) put strains on my personal schedule, so I opted to retire from teaching in December of 2021.

Favorite activities: Having the free time to spend with those who need support and assisting those in need is important to me. Having concrete accomplishments to "show" is how I spend my personal time. I create hand-painted paper flowers, do quilting, needlework (knit, crochet, embroidery, sewing) and beading. I also read a great deal. My memorable travels have included Greece, Aruba, Switzerland, Liechtenstein, Ireland, Nassau the Bahamas, a River Cruise on the Danube (from Budapest to Prague), California, and Las Vegas.

Marian influence: I commuted from Shrewsbury and worked part-time after school at Spag's, so I didn't have a great deal of "free time" or "local" access to events at Marian per se. However, I do recall numerous plays put on with St. John's and Notre Dame. Fun activities. Academically, a few moments stand out….

Mr. Gravel – Algebra – My not being able to "bust" a C+ in spite of it all…. But, I had a great foundation in Algebra that helped to develop a love of mathematics.

Mr. Bonin – Latin – structuring of classes and languages (and using my sentence diagramming skills) provided a basis for an expanded vocabulary and some rudimentary skills in other foreign languages.

Mr. Fortin – French – During my 3rd year…. I could easily read French but fell woefully short on understanding audio/oral French… Couldn't follow audio instructions but could "ace" a paper test (I think he thought I was cheating).

And I can't remember the Sister's name (so very sorry!) – Taught Freshman Physical Science and Senior Chemistry. I'm pretty sure she would remember the incident in the freshman lab regarding the Bunsen burner that wouldn't light. I asked for her help and as she tried to light it, the hose fell of the nozzle and became almost a blowtorch!!! It wasn't anyone's fault but I felt horrified! Then, I ended up signing into her Chemistry class my Senior year….bet she was thrilled to see me (though I don't remember any further "events"….)

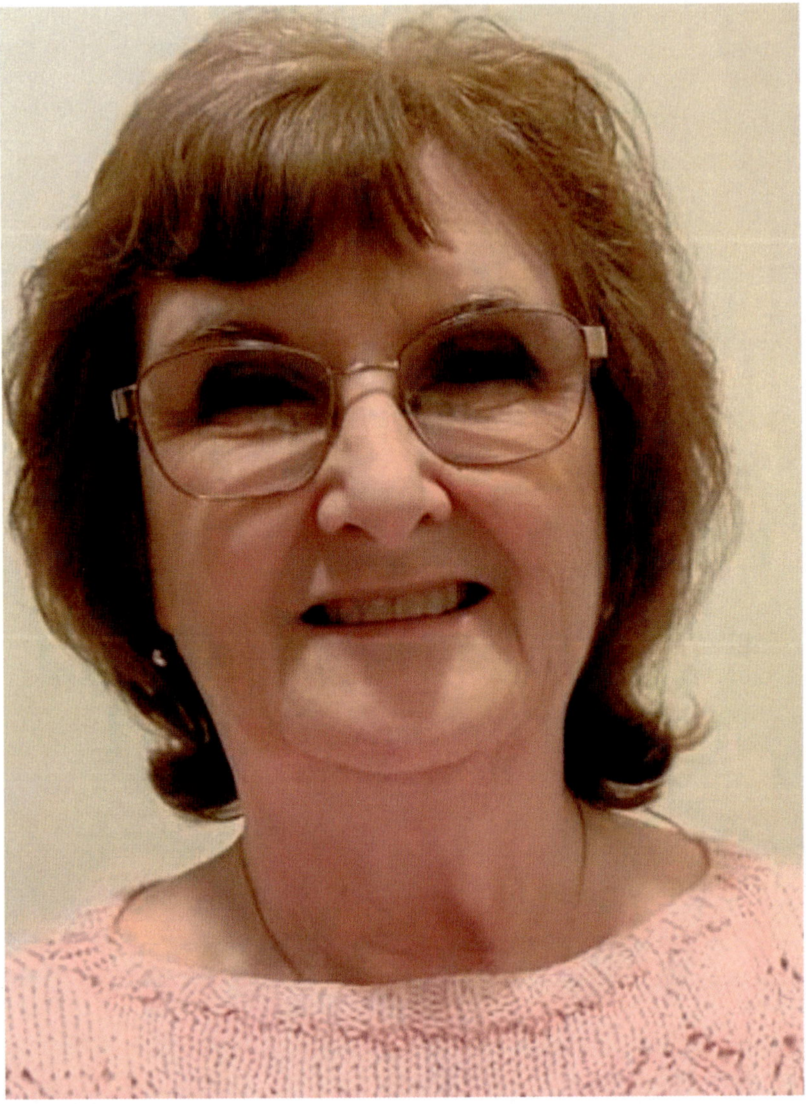

*Wisdom is not a product of schooling,
But of the lifelong attempt to acquire it."
- Albert Einstein*

Susan Athy

sxathy@gmail.com
202-270-6808
Alexendria, VA

I regret that I will not see everyone back in Worcester for the Big 50. I am amazed by the hard work that many of our classmates have put into this reunion. Thank you!

I have been living in Old Town, Alexandria, VA, with my husband and two children, for decades. I attended Georgetown undergraduate business school and law school at night. I love the Washington DC area and all it offers culturally but miss Worcester and Cape Cod. I worked for the government starting in college in 1975, as a Congressional intern, and retired in January 2023, as a Committee counsel, with a break for 8 years in between. Much of my time was spent in the areas of taxation and oversight and I was so very lucky to have worked for, and with, able and generous Members and mentors.

I think Marian provided a great foundation for my career in many ways including its strong Math program (thanks, Mr. Gravel) and its required typing course (an unexpectedly beneficial skill). As I get older, I really appreciate all the opportunities that I have had and how many nice and generous people have been a part of my life. Frankly, I do not remember many specifics about high school, except the kindness of friends, and I am fascinated (and entertained) by the detailed stories from my classmates. Hopefully, the reunion will be a chance to share fond memories and reconnect with friends.

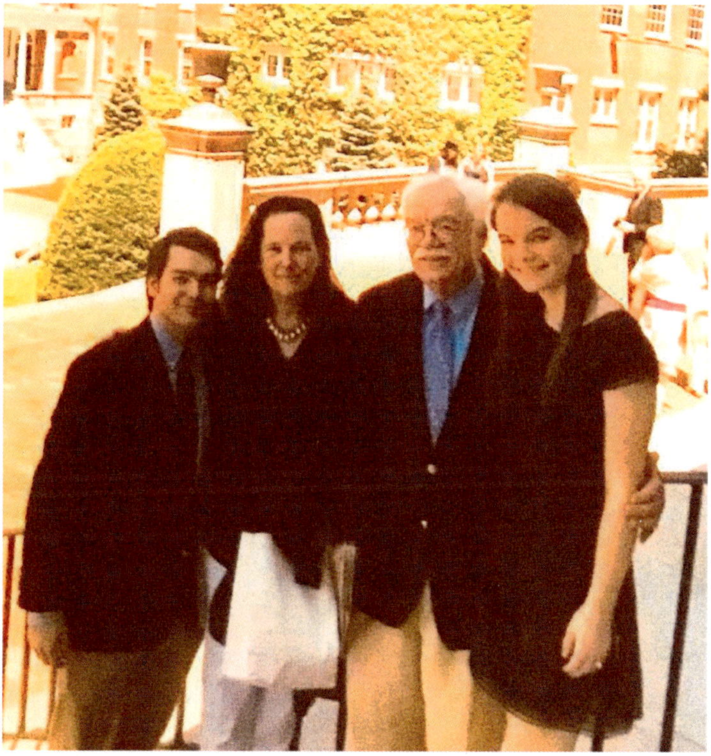

Taryn McCarthy

tarynj.mccarthy@comcast.net
857-214-1409
Rye, NH

After graduating from Marian, I went to Pine Manor College in Brookline, MA. I received an Associate Degree. I moved to Portsmouth, New Hampshire shortly after graduation and have been now living in Rye, NH for the past 13 years. I married a wonderful man and we adopted our daughter from China 28 years ago. I have two great stepsons and four grandchildren.

We love living on the seacoast and enjoy our walks along the coast. I am still in touch with a few of our classmates and look forward to seeing everyone on September 15th.

101

Teresa Mary Perodeau Doyle

teresadoyle@hotmail.com
508-450-6527
Worcester, MA

After Marian High I went to school at David Hale Fanning School of Health Occupations for the Medical Assistant Program. After graduation I started working for Physicians Bessette, Kocot, and Morse as their EKG assistant. I ended up staying in that office until 1989. Not in the same position, but actually moving up to office manager working under Lucille Pohley, MD.

I was married in 1981 to James Doyle and we had two beautiful daughters, and now two wonderful grandsons.

I love gardening, crafting, and traveling. I love music of all kinds and will go to any concert if you will go with me. □

I have been to Aruba several times, Bermuda, Spain, Hawaii, California, and Italy.

Right now my life is nice and quiet. No rushing off to work or any type of time table I need to stick to.

There you have the best parts of my life in a nutshell.

103

Therese McKeon Logan

thereselogan995@gmail.com
Huntertown, IN

Following graduation from Marian I attended yet another women's school, Emmanuel College in Boston. Once graduated, I pursued a career in Human Resources in Boston and later on the North Shore. It was during this time, I met my husband, Peter. We married in 1985, moved to the North Shore and soon after adopted our daughter and son from South Korea. We subsequently moved to Shrewsbury where we lived for the next 25 years. Once the children were in school, I began working in the Shrewsbury Public Schools as an Instructional Aid which eventually led to a 16-year position as a Preschool Teacher. I also worked in tandem as the Administrative Support for the food rescue organization, Rachel's Table in Worcester.

Upon retirement four years ago, during the height of Covid, my husband and I sold our home in Shrewsbury and took a leap of faith moving 1,000 miles away to his home town of Fort Wayne, Indiana. We have a lot of family and friends here as well as our daughter, son-in-law and 10-month-old grandson. We also take every chance we can to connect with our son who currently resides in Westborough. Peter and I have been given the opportunity to care for our grandson during the work week. We also spend time at the Y and have recently joined the pickleball craze. We enjoy "Lake Life" and are planning a family trip to South Korea next Spring.

I will always feel a sense of gratitude that I had the good fortune to spend my high school years "atop a hill for all to see" where I was given a great education and developed lifelong friendships.

105

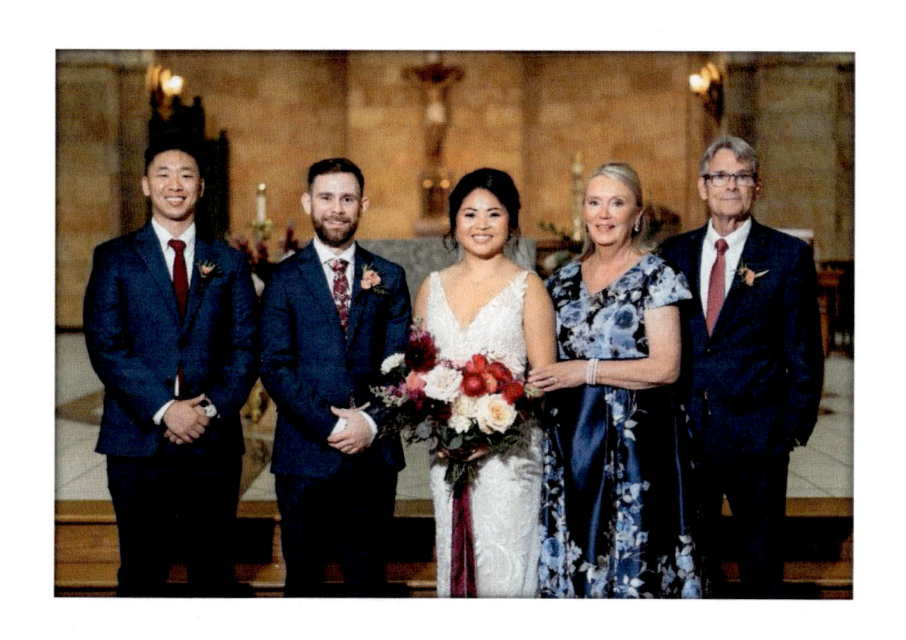

Wendy Curtis Clarke

wendy_evans@yahoo.com
207-939-5078
Freeport, Maine

Personal: Divorced and remarried, 3 children (Ben, Mike, and Jeannie), 4 granddaughters. All my kids are married and soon they will all be living in California.

Education: I grew up mostly in the Indian Lake section of Greendale. I went to Andover St. School for kindergarten and then West Boylston Street School. Forest Grove Jr. High and then Marian '74! Parish: Immaculate Conception.
Boston College '78
UConn Graduate School of Social Work '85
Smith College Graduate School of Social Work post grad 2011 (End of Life Care)
ACE Certified Personal Trainer 2018

Work Life: My early career was working in the field of developmental disabilities in Massachusetts. (WAARC, DMH, UMass Medical Center, all in Worcester and then Early Intervention in South Norfolk County). When we moved to Maine I stayed at home to raise the kids and worked at a variety of part-time jobs (some social work, some substitute teaching). In 2010, I went back to school to become a Hospice Social Worker. I provided both in-home and facility based care in Maine, Florida and NH until 2017. In 2018, I became a certified Personal Trainer, my "retirement job". I initially worked at the Exeter, NH YMCA and now I work at the Casco Bay YMCA. There, I work with individual clients and also teach Adaptive Movement classes for Seniors, members with Parkinson's Disease, and other mobility issues.

Other Stuff: I try to get outside as much as I can and Maine is a good place for that. I play a lot of tennis. I have done long distance walking events. I travel quite a bit to see my kids and other friends and family. I read a lot of nonfiction, go to a lot of museums and probably watch too much TV! I also love restaurants, again, too much!

It seems that many people say that they really didn't like High School. I did. I have such fond memories of those days. I liked that we came from all parts of the city and surrounding areas. Many of us came from working class families, me included, and I liked that. It felt familiar. It felt accepting. I hope I get to see some old friends in September. I'm looking forward to it. Thank you.

When you change your mind,

You change the world.

-Cyndi Lauper

CLASS WILL

Class Will

Maryann Abasciano leaves still talking in A flat.

Carol Ankstitus leaves a lot of friends.

Audrey Asselta leaves with Rose Candito.

Susan Athy leaves her Tab and Graham crackers to any underclassman trying to keep in shape.

Mary Beth Barnicle leaves having found "the most handsome guy" for the fifth time.

Rosemary Beahn leaves in the dust of her new ten-speed bike.

Susan Belanger leaves her parking space at Wayside.

Donna Berard leaves Lance to some hungry freshman.

Nancy Bishop leaves all her past lovers to anyone who can handle them.

Theresa Boudreau leaves for Dunkin' Donuts to calm her nerves.

Patricia Boulay, alias Bea Butt, leaves her raffle enterprise to any scheming freshman.

Kathleen Brewer leaves saying "What are they doing in there, I have to be back for night duty."

Beverly Brown leaves still wondering what she did on May 3rd.

Anne Burke leaves still wondering "How do you really get to Worcester?"

Katherine Burns leaves with trash, but no cash.

Marie Cadigan leaves still trying to convince everyone red heads have more fun.

Geralyn Callahan leaves with swollen eyes for the Naval Base to see Lemont.

Judith Camosse leaves her wire to May Abasciano for future use.

Anne Canavan leaves only to join McGovern in his next campaign.

Rosemarie Candito leaves saying, "I'd rather be dead than red in the head."

Celeste Carlson leaves with Wally.

Anne Clancy leaves with Harry J. one hour early.

Anne Clark leaves losing her tennis game to the wall.

Maura Conlin leaves her secluded spot on the path free of disgusting litter.

Rosemary Cooney leaves her special seat in the Blarney Stone, Boynton, the Pub, Lietrums, Steeples, Zachary's, etc., etc., to any thirsty junior.

Donna Corrao leaves saying, "Give me those keys!"

Linda Corriere leaves her pen marks on everyone.

Maureen Corrigan leaves to St. Anslems with her radio, TV, quiet stereo, Angel Treads, and of course, her mommy.

Maureen Cronin leaves saying, "Does anyone want a lifesaver?"

Ellen Crowley leaves for her homeland China, with Glen Campbell.

Stephanie Cullen leaves still fiddling with her rings.

Wendy Lou Curtis leaves her Marian skirt, and ribbon collection to some neat junior.

Rosemary Deedy leaves in a red Opel.

Mary Ellen Delude leaves saying, "I'm sorry, I'm sorry, I'm sorry."

Susan Denning leaves KILLER to any ready, willing, and able underclassman.

Susan Duggan leaves Charlie some free time especially from 7:30 in the morning to 2:17 in the afternoon.

Diann Erickson leaves as the Countess.

Maureen Errede leaves with corn chowder in a basket.

Patricia Fennell leaves with a stereo from the mystery man at Rye Beach.

Anne Foley leaves as the first Marian girl to have started a friendship with the Kennedys through magazines, books, TV, newspapers, etc.

Suellen Ford leaves as a pilot in a bakery. Taking dough from here and piling it over there. Then she got bored and went on the loaf.

Joan Gallagher leaves chasing who's?

Nancy Gardiner leaves as Marian's own Mary Tyler Moore.

Paula Garrepy leaves with Joan to streak in New Hampshire.

Maryellen Garvey leaves singing the theme to the "Big Valley".

Kathy Geran leaves still talking about her TECH weekend in every class.

Catherine Gleason leaves as queen of the Pub.

Patricia Goodney leaves her three course lunches to any starving junior.

Mary Grady leaves for Ireland.

Rita Grady leaves with Mary, one more time.

Kathleen Grant leaves all red.

Sheila Grogan leaves headed toward St. Stephen's court.

Felicia Gulachanski leaves saying, "Hubert!".

Ann Marie Haggerty leaves with an excuse for Miss Grady.

Kathleen Hally leaves still knitting her bikini.

Cynthia Hanley leaves a few bruises.

Kathleen Hanlon leaves not with her hope chest, but chest hopes.

Lynda Dykas leaves with a worn out knife and extra money.

Christine Harding leaves as Miss Betty Crocker.

Janice Harrington leaves with people saying, "not another red shirt, Janice."

Mary Ann Harrington leaves in her Mustang in search of some Holden action.

Maryann Harrity leaves with 155 pounds of Chuckles.

Kathleen Hart leaves us wondering whatever happened to David, Jeff, Jimmy, Rick, John, Peter, and Jack.

Mary Herman leaves the cafeteria with one less knob on the candy machine.

Mary Hudson leaves the same way she always comes in — on Fridays.

Lynn Hudson leaves G period on Monday, B period on Tuesday, F period on Wednesday, D period on Thursday — Lynn, are those all studies?

Christine Johnson leaves after using 12 tons of Clearsil and 12 gallons of Noxema.

Patricaia Johnson leaves with her thumb out heading for San Francisco looking for a free ride.

Colleen Kane leaves as Nellie with her Nellie bag, cleaning up and leaving in her yellow taxi.

Elizabeth Karras leaves saying, "Martha, which lane am I supposed to be in?"

Martha Keenan leaves her multitude of impersonations to some talented underclassman.

Maryellen Keenan leaves still having a great time at all the proms.

Patricia Kerby leaves saying to Chris Johnson, "I'll do it if you'll do it."

Nancy Kane leaves her erotic interpretations of every novel she's ever read, even the "Doll's House" Nancy?

Jean Kokernak leaves to become a Purdue chick.

Joan Ladner leaves on a regular basis.

Noreen Lahair leaves still saying, "I want to be mature."

Joanne Lavallee leaves with her famous saying, "Alright you guys, will you stop it — Come on!"

Rosalie Lawless leaves with one cigarette in her mouth, two in her hand, another behind her ear, and five packs on her dashboard.

Mary Leahy leaves her quiet manner to any deserving junior.

Karen Lee leaves Marian saying, "What? I missed that."

Andrea Legacy leaves with an endless supply of manhunt routines.

Carol Lohman leaves as Clairol — "Does she or doesn't she?"

Robin Loughlin leaves calling her mother for her term paper, her basketball uniform, her gym shirt, "Robin, do you have your cap and gown?"

Donna Lyons leaves her extra French classes to any student who can handle them.

Maryan Mangini leaves all her scarves to some longnecked junior.

Carol Martin does leave because she is still in the car hiding from her quarterly.

Debra Martin leaves her mounds to any underclassman who thinks she's deprived.

Mary Martin leaves as a friend to many.

Ann Mathews leaves Sr. Mary Claudia without a lab maid.

Taryn McCarthy leaves driving Paxton Rattles III to Forest Market one more time.

Dolores McDermott leaves looking for greener grass.

Jill McGrath leaves living on Vitamin C and Coke.

Therese McKeon leaves Scot-free.

Jean McLoughlin leaves with best wishes from the entire class.

Kathleen McMahon leaves her apple picking bag in Locker 171, her desert boots in Locker 172, and books from September to May in Locker 173.

Mary McQueen leaves at 11:19.

Mary Menanson leaves her cheerful personality and quick stories to some deserving sophomore.

Carol Menard leaves with Pat.

Joan Metivier leaves with her distiguished walk.

Lindsay Miller leaves as the "great white whale".

Cheryl Moisan leaves as she came in, with "Tee".

Mary Moloney leaves this joint.

Michelle Montville leaves her size 11 shoe to anyone who can fit it.

Susan Moylan leaves her can of Tab behind.

Mary Murphy leaves her Mark Eden course to anyone desperate enough.

Kathleen Naughton leaves saying, "You can pay me on the installment plan — 50¢ a week until the ticket is paid for."

Margaret Naughton isn't leaving — she's still asleep in the Health Room.

Sally Nawn leaves the Nola Drive Concert House for another Gumby tour.

Ann O'Brien leaves singing "Sunny".

Carolyn O'Keefe leaves saying, "But I just don't think it's right."

Michelle O'Neil leaves if she ever gets here.

Christine Parulis leaves saying, "I didn't know it was due today."

Teresa Perodeau leaves her microphone to Barbara Streisand

Mary Phelan leaves her bowling partner to any freshman interested in a French kick.

Deborah Raad has already left — "how many dismissals does that make Deb?"

Nancy Regis leaves with a smile for everyone.

Mary Rice leaves saying, "Who else can I ask?"

Karen Ritchie leaves a circle of close friends from another wild Hampton Beach summer.

Kathleen Robichaud leaves fully aware of the evils of alcohol and loving every minute of it.

Theresa Roong-Ruang leaves as Ta still saying, "The American girls have too much freedom."

Catherine Rose leaves still wondering who gave her the obscene parking ticket.

Mary Ryder leaves her holiday napkins to any messy freshman.

Debra Saunders leaves her sewing ability to some unfortunate person.

Marguerite Savage leaves a happy cookie.

Patricia Sawicki leaves with Carol.

Carole Sereti leaves with her hand on your shoulders.

Cheryl Sibley leaves her uneven bangs to anyone with an ample supply of bobby pins.

Karen Steele leaves a roadrunner for a net, a net for a roadrunner, and she's still not satisfied — "what next Karen?"

Susan Stolberg leaves — the ride is over.

Suzanne Sutherland leaves Kathy.

Deborah Szerejko leaves legally.

Kathleen Trainor leaves Suzanne.

Charlotte Triboski leaves making 3 consecutive weeks of school — "Are you here today, Charlotte?"

Donna Walsh leaves with Lisa and Debby for who knows where.

Pamela Warren leaves her newspaper illustrations and many new friends.

Christine Welsh leaves saying, "I didn't say that."

Lisa Wentworth leaves her regular trips to the girls room.

Ellen Woods leaves $(SG)^2$.

Elizabeth Wright leaves feeling like a hi — "Hi, Beth."

Tara Xenos leaves to pick up a message, still hoping to hear from Danny.

Made in the USA
Columbia, SC
27 August 2024

1fc9b601-037e-48f8-96a6-b4a7af8f3e21R01